Pilgrims
on the
Sawdust Trail

SAMFORD UNIVERSITY

Beeson Divinity Studies
Timothy George, Editor

Beeson Divinity Studies is a series of volumes dedicated to the pastoral and theological renewal of the Church of Jesus Christ. The series is sponsored by the faculty of Beeson Divinity School of Samford University, an evangelical, interdenominational theological school in Birmingham, Alabama.

Pilgrims
on the
Sawdust Trail

EVANGELICAL ECUMENISM
AND THE QUEST FOR CHRISTIAN IDENTITY

Timothy George, EDITOR

Foreword by Mark A. Noll

Baker Academic
Grand Rapids, Michigan

Published by Baker Academic
a division of Baker Publishing Group
P.O. Box 6287, Grand Rapids, MI 49516-6287
www.bakeracademic.com

Printed in the United States of America

Library of Congress Cataloging-in-Publication Data
Pilgrims on the sawdust trail : evangelical ecumenism and the quest
  for Christian identity / Timothy George, editor.
        p.   cm.
    Includes bibliographical references and index.
    ISBN 0-8010-2764-0 (pbk.)
    1. Evangelicalism. I. George, Timothy.
BR1640.P55 2004
270.8'3—dc22   2003063902

for

Avery Cardinal Dulles, S.J.
and
James Inell Packer

theologians of unity-in-truth,
exemplars of Baxterian wisdom:

in necessariis unitas,
in non-necessariis libertas,
in utrisque caritas

Contents

Foreword

American Past and World Present in the Search for Evangelical Identity

Mark A. Noll

Pilgrims on the Sawdust Trail offers a well-chosen series of informative, sympathetic, and passionate snapshots of American evangelicals at the start of the twenty-first century. Like a good family photo album, the pictures are a bit jumbled. By viewing the evangelical family from different angles, the various authors/photographers highlight much for which modest pride is justifiable, but there are also in view enough eccentrics, curmudgeons, oddities, and signs of hastily hidden strife to keep things realistic. Most of all, this mosaic portrait offers much evidence to confirm the fluid and dynamic character of American evangelicalism itself. Things are changing, and they are changing fast.

Thus, in this single book, we find an extraordinary range of constructive dialogue: evangelical-fundamentalist, evangelical-pentecostal, evangelical–Roman Catholic, evangelical-ecumenical, and evangelical–mainline Protestant. But even to list the contents in this way is enough to cause a little head-scratching. Doesn't everyone simply take for granted that fundamentalists, pentecostals, and many mainline Protestants are subsets of the evangelical mosaic? If the ecumenical challenge offered below by Gabriel Fackre to evangelicals, which focuses on the mandates of the gospel for all Christians, is taken to heart, don't we come away with another bending of rigid categories? And what about the evangelical-Catholic exchange, represented here by the Southern Baptist Timothy George and by the Catholics Richard John Neuhaus and Brother Jeffrey Gros? If theological Rip Van Winkles who fell asleep only a few short decades ago would take the contents of the exchange seriously, they might conclude they had awoken on a different planet. The ferment to which these chapters speak, as well as the maturing of evangelical identities that they also document, might profitably be illuminated by a little history as well as by a consideration of what, even with the wide coverage of its themes, the book leaves out.

For much of the nineteenth century, white evangelical Protestants constituted the largest and most influential body of religious adherents in the United States (as also in Britain and Canada). Methodists, Baptists, Presbyterians, Congregationalists, and many Episcopalians shared broadly evangelical convictions—though they could battle each other aggressively on the details of those convictions. Evangelical elements were also prominent among Lutherans, German and Dutch Reformed, and the Restorationist churches (Churches of Christ, Disciples of Christ).

Division in the Protestant tradition—especially the fundamentalist-modernist battles of the first quarter of the twentieth century—greatly weakened the public presence of evangelicalism. At about the same time, large-scale immigration of non-Protestants, the growth of cities as multicultural sites, and the secularization of higher education also eroded evangelical cultural influence. The passing of evangelical cultural dominance, however, was also accompanied by significant new developments. The most important of these was the emergence of Pentecostalism, which began early in the twentieth century as an outgrowth of emphases on Christian "holiness" in several Protestant bodies. And that development, as is now well known, has had world historical significance.

During the Great Depression and the Second World War, evangelicalism was less visible than it has ever been, before or since, in American life. The fundamentalist strand of evangelicalism promoted "separation" from the world and the construction of a self-contained network of churches, publishers, Bible schools, colleges, and radio broadcasting (in which fundamentalists were the pioneers for religious purposes). Out of sight of media elites and against the trend of the older Protestant groups, several evangelical denominations—including the Southern Baptist Convention, Assemblies of God, the Church of God in Christ, and the Christian and Missionary Alliance—grew rapidly in the 1930s and '40s. In roughly the same period, fundamentalists and evangelicals established new connections with a number of immigrant traditions, like the Dutch-American Christian Reformed Church and several Mennonite denominations, that would later play a large role in post–World War II evangelical enterprises. It was often itinerating evangelists or radio broadcasts—like those emanating from the Moody Bible Institute in Chicago—that made these connections.

The three decades from the end of World War II to the mid-1970s marked a distinct era in American evangelical history. The prominent public activity of the evangelist Billy Graham inspired many fundamentalists and evangelicals, especially in the North, even as it recruited new adherents for evangelical causes and created coalitions beyond previous evangelical boundaries. Postwar "neo-evangelicalism," a phrase popular in the 1950s and '60s to describe former fundamentalists who sought a positive public image, was, however, considerably more than Billy Graham. When Graham downplayed issues central to earlier fundamentalist-modernist strife and set aside some fundamentalist shibboleths, many were eager to follow. During the war itself, these leaders founded the National Association of Evangelicals in 1942 to handle relations with the government and promote transdenominational cooperation. Soon the combined efforts of institutional leaders like Harold John Ockenga, intellectuals like Carl F. H. Henry, wealthy laymen like Herbert J. Taylor of Club Aluminum and J. Howard Pew of Sun Oil, along with a host of missionary-minded young people, led to the creation or expansion of many ventures in education, publishing, and youth work. As part of this same surge, self-identified evangelicals soon made up the largest component of missionaries sent from the United States to other parts of the world.

Since the early 1970s the diversity that always existed within American evangelicalism has become much more obvious. With many evangelicals, reactions to major social convulsions, like racial conflict, the women's movement, and sexual permissiveness, have sparked a rebirth of political activism. Many new religious developments, including the charismatic movement, the decline of denominations, and the growth of parachurch networks, have also influenced recent evangelical history.

Recent decades have also witnessed a repositioning of old antagonisms. The increasing frequency and depth of dialogue between evangelicals and Roman Catholics is the most prominent sign of such changes. But evangelicals have also helped once-sectarian groups like the Seventh-day Adventists and the Worldwide Church of God move toward more traditional Christian affirmations. At the end of the twentieth century, there were even a few signs of improved relations between some evangelicals and Mormons, whom most evangelicals had long considered far beyond the pale.

What such a history, sketched so briefly here, means for the future of evangelical self-identity is the theme of Joel Carpenter's chapter, which does its job very well indeed. But in reflecting on the shape of evangelical identity, it is very important to think as broadly as possible, which the essays by George D. McKinney and Cheryl Bridges Johns especially help readers in doing. They highlight the question of black-white relations among evangelicals, which is a theme that leads naturally into considering the connection of American evangelicals to evangelical-like groups of many other hues that today are spread to every corner of the globe.

The relationship of African American churches to evangelical traditions is complex. Blacks in America only began to accept Christianity in the mid–eighteenth century, when the Christian message was presented to them by figures like the grand itinerant George Whitefield or the Virginia Presbyterian Samuel Davies. To this day, most African American denominations and independent congregations share many evangelical characteristics, including belief in the "new birth," trust in the Scriptures, and commitment to traditional morality. Some white evangelicals, like the student of Jonathan Edwards, Samuel Hopkins, and the founder of American Methodism, Francis Asbury, were early leaders in the fight against slavery. Yet other evangelicals, North as well as South, either tolerated or defended slavery. Throughout the nineteenth century, almost all white evangelicals also frowned on elements of African ritual retained in the worship of black Christians. That in the twentieth century white evangelicals have mostly supported the social and political status quo means that ties between black Protestants and white evangelicals are not nearly as close as their shared religious beliefs might lead an observer to expect.

If this aspect of American history poses a special challenge to the formation of an evangelical identity in which "all are one in Christ Jesus" (Gal. 3:28), the recent history of the Christian gospel around the world makes for even more to ponder. As more and more observers are pointing out, over the last century there has taken place a nearly unprecedented globalization of distinctly evangelical movements and of movements that share many evangelical features.

Whatever someone might conclude about evangelical developments in American life, the most remarkable features of the recent past have concerned other parts of the planet. Evangelicals from around the world continue to come to Britain, the United States, and Canada for training, but so now do missionaries from the Two-Thirds World arrive to spread the gospel among fellow immigrants in the West, and also to evangelize among Western pagans. The newer evangelical churches of the world face many difficulties of their own—instability, lack of wise leadership, shortage of educational materials, ethnic violence, numbing poverty, and more. Yet from these churches are now flowing insights, practices, songs, and doctrinal emphases back toward the original evangelical homelands.

According to authoritative missiological estimates, in 1900 well over 90 percent of the world's evangelical Christians lived in Europe or North America. But because of a number of factors—Western missionary activity, cooperative efforts at translating the Bible into local languages, the dedicated efforts of national Christians in many parts of the world, and developments in worldwide trade and communication—that earlier situation has been dramatically transformed. Today, at least by some definitions of the term, the number of evangelicals in *each* of Africa, Latin America, and Asia exceeds the total in Europe and

North America *combined*. Increasingly, the personnel that most effectively contribute to the spread of evangelical Christianity are recruited from the southern rather than the northern hemisphere. Today, for example, Campus Crusade for Christ, International, employs more than 15,000 workers around the world, with only about 1,000 from the United States. It is the same with Youth with a Mission, a church-planting agency with about 12,000 workers, of whom less than 2,000 are from the United States, and the Wycliffe Bible translators, less than half of whose staff members are Americans.

The 2001 edition of David Barrett's *World Christian Encyclopedia* presents even more dramatic evidence about the broader changes of recent decades. Using Barrett's narrowest definition of "evangelical," the *Encyclopedia* did find that more "evangelicals" lived in the United States (40.6 million) than anywhere else in the world, but also that, one hundred years ago, almost no evangelicals existed in the next most populous "evangelical" countries: Brazil (27.7 million) and Nigeria (22.3 million). Of the next four countries where Barrett found the largest number of evangelicals, one was a historical center of evangelical strength (the United Kingdom, 11.6 million), but three had witnessed the growth of substantial evangelical populations, mostly in the past century (India, 9.3 million; South Korea, 9.1 million; South Africa, 9.1 million). Of the remaining twenty-four countries where Barrett found at least one million evangelicals, only three were in Europe (Germany, Romania, Ukraine) and one in North America (Canada). Fully ten of these others were in Africa (Angola, Congo-Zaire, Ethiopia, Ghana, Kenya, Mozambique, Rwanda, Tanzania, Uganda, Zambia), five were in Asia (China, Myanmar, Indonesia, Philippines, Australia), and five were in Latin America (Guatemala, Haiti, Mexico, Argentina, Peru). If to these totals were added the numbers in evangelical-like groups, or in movements decisively influenced by fundamentalists, evangelicals, pentecostals, or pietists, the totals would be several times as high.

Contemporary efforts to describe the current course and the future of evangelicalism must be impressionistic, since the phenomenon designated by the word represents flexible beliefs and practices rather than sharply defined organizations. Serious students of evangelical identity have long recognized that evangelicalism is not an organized religious movement as such, but rather an ever-diversifying series of local churches, parachurch agencies, national and international ministries, and interlocking networks of publications, preachers, and personal contacts.

For the future, it is likely that the patterns of the past will continue. Relatively small numbers of individuals and agencies, often active in networks of voluntary societies or mission agencies, will self-consciously label themselves and their efforts as evangelical. Much larger numbers will be associated with churches and other institutions embedded securely in the historical evangelical movements. And still larger numbers from throughout the world, who may have only loose connections with original evangelical movements, will nonetheless continue to uphold the historic beliefs and practices of evangelicalism.

The challenges ahead for evangelical identity will differ considerably depending on where evangelicals are located. For those in the former heartlands of Britain and North America, it will be a continuing labor to retain the historical evangelical combination of classical Protestant theology and effective popular outreach. A few evangelicals are always tempted toward scholastic orthodoxies, but in so doing become alienated from contemporary culture as self-enclosed sectarian cliques. A more extensive danger is that the historic evangelical populism will degenerate into mere accommodation to contemporary society, especially to the therapeutic demands of a consumer culture. Especially for questions of American evangelical identity, problems remain concerning the ability to sustain intellectual vigor in an environment in which evangelical subcultures easily run off into escapist literature (especially novels about the return of Christ), political extremism (usually of the Right), polemical science (especially scientific creationism), and affective anti-intellectualism (especially in some of the modern praise songs).

Increasingly, however, the future of American evangelical identity will likely be tied more closely to what happens in the rest of the world. Throughout the southern hemisphere, the evangelical gospel message has worked wonders by providing hope and fellowship with God. And yet many uncertainties remain, some having to do with problems of social construction, some relating to strife with Islamic, Hindu, and native religions, and still more concerning the collapse of once-secure local cultures in the face of world economic and political assimilation.

For all evangelicals it will remain a challenge to maintain classical traditions of trinitarian theological orthodoxy while absorbing the excitements of pentecostal and charismatic faith. The ideal will be for traditional evangelicals to be quickened by movements of the Holy Spirit and for devotees of the Spirit to learn balance and gravity from the traditionalists. But the traditional strengths of evangelical theology could be blown away by winds of the Spirit, and new pentecostal groups might come to imitate the deadening formalism and enervating moralism that have sometimes characterized the older evangelical movements.

Concerns for the future of evangelicalism—and hence also for evangelical identity—center on whether its informal networks of communication can provide the discipline, the self-correction, and the connectedness that, at its best, have marked the history of the movement. Through the critical agents of transmission—voluntary associations (e.g., Bible societies and mission agencies), personal ties, widely read books, pace-setting periodicals, hymns (by older authors and new)—evangelicalism has remained not only relatively cohesive, but relatively faithful to the Christian gospel. These agents and strategies of communication that once defined the character of evangelicalism in the regions of the North Atlantic have now spread around the world. On their resilience would seem to hang the future of the movement. Readers who ponder seriously the chapters of this book will be in a much better position to gauge such prospects for themselves.

Introduction

Timothy George

During the past generation, American evangelicals have moved from the margins to the mainstream of religious life in the United States. This shift has brought challenges and threats to evangelical identity as well as wonderful opportunities for mission and outreach. It has also brought new conversations and relationships, both among evangelicals themselves and with others long separated by theological and historical differences.

The essays in this volume were originally presented at a symposium that brought together scholars and church leaders to examine recent discussions and new initiatives among evangelicals and fundamentalists, evangelicals and pentecostals, evangelicals and Roman Catholics, and evangelicals and mainline Protestants. Our desire was to speak to one another, not merely about one another. Underlying these discussions was a common conviction, namely, that the New Testament imperative of speaking the truth in love would lead, by God's grace, to greater mutual understanding and to a deeper faithfulness to Jesus Christ. The participants in these conversations were not seeking a false unity that ignores differences of conviction and conscience. But out of these conversations we have gained a greater appreciation for one another as fellow believers in Jesus Christ, for the unity that we share as members of the body of Christ as well as for the burdensome joy of dialogue—which requires listening as well as speaking, and receiving as well as giving—in the service of the church, for the furtherance of the faith, to the glory of God alone.

Joel A. Carpenter is provost of Calvin College and a distinguished historian of American fundamentalism and evangelicalism. In "The Fellowship of Kindred Minds: Evangelical Identity and the Quest for Christian Unity," Carpenter reviews the historical impulses that contributed to the rise of evangelicalism. He also discusses the divisive character of the evangelical movement as a contrarian witness within the Protestant tradition as well as various unitive forces that have also marked the evangelical experience. This is an important keynote essay that explains, in part, why dialogue has historically been so difficult for evangelicals and why it still remains controversial for many today.

Contemporary American evangelicalism emerged out of a biblicistic movement of reaction and retrenchment commonly called fundamentalism. The first major section of the book examines this relationship from both sides of this historical divide. Richard J. Mouw is president of Fuller Theological Seminary and author of *The Smell of Sawdust,* part memoir, part critical appraisal of his own experience in the fundamentalist subculture. In "What Evangelicals Can Learn from Fundamentalists" Mouw explains why many conservative Protestant Christians felt it necessary to distance themselves from some of the harsher elements of the fundamentalist heritage, but he also expresses appreciation for other elements in this tradition that he thinks have been too easily discarded. He calls for evangelicals to recover—through a "second naïveté"—new appreciation and fresh engagement with the better impulses of the fundamentalist phenomenon without lapsing into the legalism, anti-intellectualism, and separatism that have marred the movement. Kevin T. Bauder, professor of systematic theology at Central Baptist Theological Seminary, a historic fundamentalist school in Minnesota, responds to Mouw's appeal with civility and gratitude but also resistance. For all Mouw's goodwill, Bauder thinks that he has misunderstood and "ever so slightly stereotyped" the fundamentalism Bauder embraces. Bauder makes a strong appeal for the *idea* of fundamentalism with its concern for the purity of the visible church. Rightly seen in this light, fundamentalism remains a viable force in church life today related, as Bauder argues it is, to the centrality of the gospel rather than the negotiable boundaries of Christian fellowship.

Both Pentecostalism and fundamentalism arose in the early twentieth century and share a number of features, including a strong biblical commitment, a countercultural ecclesiology, and an emphasis on a distinctive Christian lifestyle. Pentecostals are frequently classified as evangelicals in demographic surveys of the world Christian movement. Pentecostals have been active participants and leaders in the National Associations of Evangelicals from its inception in 1942. At the same time, there has been great tension between pentecostals and evangelicals, and many pentecostals have felt marginalized in evangelical councils, publications, and institutions. Bishop George D. McKinney is senior pastor of St. Stephen's Church of God in Christ in San Diego, a scholar-activist well known for his interdenominational and ecumenical commitments. In "The Azusa Street Revival Revisited," Bishop McKinney takes us back to the origins of the American pentecostal movement in the Los Angeles revival of 1907. He focuses particularly on the witness of W. J. Seymour, the leading figure in that movement. Seymour organized the first intentionally interracial congregation in the United States. Thus McKinney examines the pentecostal witness in light of concerns for racial reconciliation and justice. A participant in recent efforts to transcend the legacy of segregation within the pentecostal tradition, McKinney interprets Azusa as a model for the recovery of the vision of unity and justice symbolized in Seymour's mantra of the "washing away of the color line in the blood of Jesus."

Cheryl Bridges Johns, speaking from the perspective of a historically white pentecostal denomination (the Church of God, Cleveland, Tennessee), responds with appreciation to McKinney's vision, adding a distinctive word about gender reconciliation. Johns has also been an active participant in the recent Roman Catholic–pentecostal dialogue and thinks that pentecostals have much to offer to the ecumenical quest: "Within Pentecostalism there is a 'subversive memory' of a vision of Christian unity. It is a vision found among those who long ago walked a sawdust trail toward a new order of creation." In his sermonic essay "Who Is the Holy Spirit for Us Today?" Glenn E.

Davis examines some of the reasons why certain evangelicals (and fundamentalists) have resisted the pentecostal witness as misguided or even dangerous. Speaking from his personal experience as a minister in the Charismatic Episcopal tradition, he examines a key biblical passage on spiritual renewal and calls for a reconsideration and new engagement across this historic divide.

As evangelicalism emerged from the post-fundamentalist context of post–World War II conservative Protestantism, it positioned itself polemically against two fronts: Protestant liberalism (often called modernism back then) and pre–Vatican II Roman Catholicism. In recent years, however, many evangelicals and Roman Catholics have discovered that they share many things and have begun to make common cause on several fronts. One of the leaders in this effort is Richard John Neuhaus, editor-in-chief of *First Things* and a former Lutheran priest who converted to Roman Catholicism in 1990. In 1994, Neuhaus and Chuck Colson launched the initiative known as Evangelicals and Catholics Together. In "Why Evangelicals and Catholics Belong Together," Neuhaus reviews this initiative and projects a hopeful scenario for future Roman Catholic and evangelical engagement. Jeffrey Gros is an ecumenical officer with the National Council of Catholic Bishops. He reviews various Roman Catholic and evangelical discussions, including Evangelicals and Catholics Together (ECT) and the Roman Catholic–pentecostal dialogue, and calls for a "common witness" despite significant persisting differences. Timothy George, dean of Beeson Divinity School of Samford University and an active participant in the ECT process, examines evangelical motivations for engagement with Roman Catholics and also addresses some of the issues raised by evangelical critics of such efforts.

Gabriel Fackre and Thomas C. Oden are leading theologians with significant experience in both the evangelical and ecumenical camps. Fackre thinks evangelicals and ecumenicals have much to learn from one another, as well as things to be wary about in one another's traditions, and he offers a winsome and hopeful prospect for a greater confluence between these two communities. Oden, on the other hand, offers the paradigm of "a new ecumenism," one that bypasses the official ecumenical and denominational structures of the older Protestant establishment in favor of new alliances and emerging associations of like-minded believers committed to the historic Christian faith.

The essays by Zahl, Knippers, and Armstrong remind us of the Reformation principle of *ecclesia semper reformanda*—the church reformed and yet ever reforming on the basis of the Word of God. John Calvin once said that "the building of the church must still be combined with many struggles."[1] The very idea of pilgrimage, the guiding motif of this book, reminds us that the church is always *in via*, not there yet, always needing to persist with humility and vigilance in the service of Jesus Christ. But pilgrimage is not a solitary concept, and the essays in this volume are an invitation to a continuing journey in process, a journey toward that City with foundations whose builder and architect is God.

Part 1

EVANGELICALS AT THE TABLE

1

The Fellowship of Kindred Minds

EVANGELICAL IDENTITY
AND THE QUEST FOR CHRISTIAN UNITY

Joel A. Carpenter

A few years ago, I heard a story about the 1991 assembly of the World Council of Churches, Australia. An aged founder of the World Council was heading toward the great assembly hall when he beheld a familiar sight. Standing there with a protest sign was another veteran, Carl McIntire, the arch-separatist fundamentalist, who had opposed the World Council since its founding days. To McIntire it was the whore of Babylon, the false church prophesied in the Book of Revelation. The two old campaigners greeted each other cordially, like senators from across the aisle. They were saying, in effect, that the assembly would not be complete without one or the other of them, for each had a role to perform.[1] There was a time, indeed, when evangelical Protestants were thought of as the sectarian pick-eters outside the places where other Christians—Protestant, Roman Catholic, and Orthodox—gather to affirm their common identity and mission and to engage in dialogue about their differences.

Increasingly in recent years, however, evangelicals have been at the table, engaging in the conversation. The World Evangelical Fellowship's Task Force on Ecumenical Issues, for example, met repeatedly during the 1990s with representatives of the Roman Catholic Council for the Promotion of Christian Unity. In the spring of 1994 another initiate led by Richard John Neuhaus produced an unofficial but highly salient statement, "Evangelicals and Catholics Together," over the signature of prominent American Catholic and evangelical leaders. Repeatedly since the Canberra Assembly, the World Council of Churches has called for a deeper engagement with evangelical and pentecostal groups. Since 1972, there have also been ecumenical discussions between Roman Catholic officials and representatives of the pentecostal tradition. In addition to traditional Protestant-Catholic tensions, these two traditions are deeply aware of each others' frequently adversarial positions on the front lines of evangelization, in the United States for sure, but most intensely in Latin America.[2]

I will never forget a session of the Evangelical Theological Consultation within the American Academy of Religion, which featured a pentecostal and Catholic dialogue on the doctrine of the Holy Spirit. I came a little late, but just in time to hear the winsome, inviting, but utterly honest thinking of a pink-faced, silver-haired Catholic lay theologian in a tweed jacket. Up next was a longtime pentecostal servant of the dialogue, Professor Mel Robeck of Fuller Theological Seminary. He kept referring to his Catholic counterpart as "Brother Jeffrey," and hearing that pentecostal term of endearment, I marveled at the warmth of fellowship. Later I found out that Brother Jeffrey Gros is actually a "brother" by title, as a member of a religious order. But to Mel and others in the room, he was Brother Jeffrey in both senses. Evangelicals of many varieties, then, including the most dynamic and influential evangelicals today, the pentecostals, are at the table, engaging in the conversation, and are there to stay for some time, I believe, regardless of the tensions and differences.

It is well worth pausing, then, to ask what evangelicals bring to the conversation of Christian identity and unity, both by way of their gifts to enhance it and their propensity to provoke intrafaith conflict. Evangelicals have built-in impatience and suspicions regarding some of the most salient movements and traditions behind contemporary ecumenism. These feelings emanate from some of evangelical Protestantism's deepest traits, and are ingrained in their identity and sense of mission. Evangelicals also bring an alternative model of ecumenical fellowship, cooperation, and mission to the conciliar model now prevailing, and this other way is well worth considering in the years to come. In this essay, then, I hope to convey some of the distinctives of evangelical identity, and to show how these traits have led evangelical movements and traditions both to be a divisive force in world Christianity, and a unitive force as well.

Evangelicals' Historic Identity

Much ink has been spilled over the past quarter-century in attempts to define *evangelicalism* and to describe the essence of this vast and varied collection of movements and traditions. In recent years, the debate over evangelical identity has turned toward whether there is in fact an "essentialist" evangelicalism that can cover all varieties. Some scholars of the holiness and pentecostal traditions have charged, in fact, that the term has been co-opted by the more Calvinistic "post-fundamentalist party" in contemporary American Protestantism.[3] This party has been led by the Carl Henry, Billy Graham, and Harold Ockenga generation that organized the National Association of Evangelicals, Fuller Theological Seminary, the World Evangelical Fellowship, the Billy Graham Evangelistic Association, and their sponsored ventures, such as *Christianity Today* magazine and the Lausanne Committee for World Evangelization. It is true that this group has enjoyed salience and leadership over the past half-century beyond what its numbers would warrant. It is also true that contemporary pentecostals and charismatics often talk of themselves as something different from these evangelicals. And it is true, I must add, that, historians' claims of neutrality to the contrary, attempts to describe cannot be separated from attempts to prescribe. In the end, however, historians and social scientists have found the "e-word" to be useful. They persist in using it in a broad way that can cover pentecostals, pietistic Lutherans, and Southern Baptists as well as the born-again citizens of Wheaton, Illinois.

Let me attempt, then, in a broad-brushed way, to describe the evangelical tradition and impulse. *Evangelical* means, quite simply, pertaining to the evangel, the good news that God redeems sinful humanity through Jesus Christ. Evangelical Protestants have stressed that people find salvation only through personal faith in Christ's atoning death and the regenerating power of the Holy Spirit. *Evangelical* also denotes an urgent drive to proclaim this gospel to others by word and deed. Variations in time and place have nuanced the term's meaning and usage and given it much historic freight.

The churches of the Lutheran Reformation first put *evangelical* into common usage, using the term to describe their distinctive features: salvation by grace alone, through faith, and the Bible as the Christian's supreme authority. In time, Germanic people equated *evangelical* with Protestant, meaning especially the Lutherans.

The Reformation doctrines of *sola fides* and *sola scriptura* still inform twentieth-century evangelical movements, but in the seventeenth century, a renewed desire for personally experienced, heartfelt, and life-transforming faith gave new content to the meaning of *evangelical.* The English Puritan movement stressed conversion, a personal experience of receiving God's grace, and downplayed the inherent saving value of liturgy and sacraments. Puritans believed that conversion infused one with zeal for God's will in all of life, which prompted them to seek reform in society and government as well as the church. The somewhat later Pietist movement on the European continent was a reaction against spiritual decline in the Lutheran and Reformed churches. Like Puritans, Pietists stressed the need for conversion, but they downplayed rationalistic and creedal definitions of religious truth, insisting that truth be validated by experience. Their "experimental" religion featured much prayer, self-denial, close fellowship, Bible study, and evangelistic zeal. The Moravians, a pietistic communal fellowship led by Count Zinzendorf, who was a Lutheran nobleman, sent missionary pioneers to many lands in the early eighteenth century.

Further elaborations on what it meant to be evangelical came during the revivals that swept Great Britain and her American colonies in the mid–eighteenth century. A group of Anglican priests led by Charles and John Wesley and George

Whitefield was convinced by the teachings of the Puritans and the Pietists that they needed to know Jesus Christ personally, and each experienced conversion. As they preached in churches, fields, and jails, the quiet witness of the Pietists and the Puritan belief that conversion usually followed a long spiritual travail were transformed. Whitefield and the Wesleys boldly urged multitudes to be "born again" that very day.

The result was a great wave of conversions, renewed religious zeal, and controversy in the mid–eighteenth century that the British called the Evangelical Revival and the Americans the Great Awakening. A strong evangelical party developed within the Church of England, which promoted a new wave of missionary endeavor and social reform. The Wesleys' ministry spawned its own cell groups and eventually the Methodist Church, which became a major liberating force among the working classes. In America, the ongoing revivals stirred all the denominations, provoking controversy, schisms, and growth. By the turn of the century, the most intensely evangelistic churches—the Baptists and Methodists—were the fastest growing. The revivals crossed all barriers in early America, most importantly, the color line. For the Africans in captivity, the gospel was good news indeed. In the emerging black Christian community, Jesus became a rock in a very weary land. Once they found the truth, the African Americans knew that this truth would set them free.

This new movement differed greatly from the "evangelical churches" of Luther's day. The evangelical persuasion now included a lessened emphasis on the creedal and sacramental channels of faith, a preference for voluntary religious affiliation and interdenominational cooperation, aggressive evangelization, conversionist views of salvation, earnest and abstemious living, and revivalistic and millennial expectations about God's work in the days to come.[4]

We all know the rest of the story, I suppose—how this tradition became the dominant one in nineteenth-century America and spawned a great variety of movements for revival, reform, and new denominations. From around the turn of the twentieth century forward, it fostered a variety of movements to revive, reform, or separate from a mainline Protestantism that evangelicals thought was growing more worldly, less firmly attached to the apostolic doctrines, and less assured of the faith's supernatural power. By the end of the twentieth century, despite their dissenting status within American Protestantism, the evangelical forms of Christianity had penetrated every Christian tradition and racial and ethnic group in North America, from African Americans to Koreans, and in each community the faith gained new shape and texture. Evangelicals developed renewal movements within every old-line Protestant denomination, plus an evangelistic movement in the Antiochian Orthodox Church, and a huge and vibrant charismatic movement within Roman Catholicism. Meanwhile, missionary activity and indigenous church development in the Global South have made the evangelical Protestant family within Christianity, and particularly the pentecostal and charismatic cousinry, the world's fastest-growing Christian tradition. Recent initiatives on the part of the World Council of Churches and the Roman Catholic communion to engage evangelicals in dialogue have come, in no small part, from recognition that this Christian persuasion cannot be ignored. Indeed, given the astonishing shifts in the centers of Christian adherence over the past fifty years, any ecumenicity that does not include evangelicals is not worthy of the name.

Engaging and including evangelical Protestants in common Christian witness can be difficult, however, to say the least. On some occasions, evangelicals appear to be the most unitive and warmly inclusive Christians around, but on others, the most sectarian and divisive. To understand why, we need some more background.

Evangelical Christianity as a Divisive Force

Pietists, Puritans, and evangelical awakeners of all sorts in modern times have started with a common premise: something is amiss in Christendom. Evangelicalism, says the mission historian Andrew Walls, "is a religion of protest against a Christian society that is not Christian enough."[5] Said early Puritans about the Church of England, it was only "halfly reformed." Said Wesley, Whitefield, and other preachers of the Great Awakening, the churches are full of unconverted people, including the ministers. This renewal impulse, with the expressed critique of the mainstream church and the society over which it presides, is a central feature of evangelical movements. Evangelicals commonly declare that the mainstream church is spiritually cold, stiltedly formal in worship, doctrinally ignorant or deviant, lacking in holiness, growing complacent and worldly, and losing the power to shape society in a Christian direction. In response, evangelicals have fostered *ecclesiolae in ecclesia*, little gatherings of the renewed and revived, who pray, study, and work for renewal. From these beginnings, greater movements have arisen, with enormous potential to agitate, disrupt, and rearrange the religious and social landscape. This element of dissent, judgment, and disruption can seem particularly self-righteous and insulting to mainstream church leaders. Repeatedly it has resulted in conflict, lingering resentment and distrust, and in many cases, formal schism.

Indeed, separatism, the principled abandoning of older ecclesial structures and the establishing of new ones, often has been the result of evangelical revivals. It is one of the great ironies of modern church history that the recurrent evangelical visions of renewal and calls for restoring the church to its primitive unity, purity, and power have resulted, repeatedly, in the founding of yet another sect. The churches of the Reformation fall into this pattern in some respects, as does the Methodist Church, which is the ironic result of the work of high-church-men John and Charles Wesley. The Disciples of Christ and Christian Churches, founded by Scottish Americans Alexander Campbell and Barton Stone in the Second Great Awakening, were more clearly antisectarian sects, as were the various contending camps of the Brethren movement of the mid– to late nineteenth century, pioneered by the Irish Anglican John Nelson Darby. Holiness, pentecostal, and fundamentalist movements over the past century have created yet more sectarian offspring, and many contemporary evangelical movements, worldwide, seem not even to bother to organize churchly ties beyond the local congregation. In the United States, these independent evangelical congregations, charismatic and otherwise, contain some four million members, far more than the United

Church of Christ and the Episcopal Church combined. One might complain, as I know that Roman Catholics do, that this is the cancerous outgrowth of the Protestant principle, and it has resulted in repeated blows against the peace and visible unity of the church.

A kindred feature of evangelical movements and traditions has been their freewheeling, entrepreneurial style and outlook. Wesley and Whitefield, and every great evangelist since them, have freely employed "new measures" to deliver the gospel message to the masses. The Awakeners took to the fields, markets, and mine faces, and these were revolutionary moves in their day. They were innovative in style and organization as well. Wesley organized networks of traveling missionaries and discipleship groups, which eventually formed the backbone of the Methodist Church. Whitefield, meanwhile, was an inventive exploiter of the day's mass media, both the newspapers and the theatrical rhetorical style. None of these new measures was sanctioned by the ecclesiastical powers; indeed, some of them were expedient fallbacks from failed attempts to win churchly support for more conventional, in-the-pulpit preaching.

This innovative style took on an institutional form in time, what we have come to call the parachurch mode of organizing the Christian mission to the world. The pioneers of the parachurch revolution were the early Protestant foreign missionary societies. They arose because, as Walls puts it, "none of the classical patterns of Church government . . . had any machinery to do the tasks for which missionary societies came into being." By their success, he continues, the voluntary societies "subverted all the classical forms of Church government, while fitting comfortably into none of them." These ecclesiastical systems, which had been worked out and argued over for centuries, and even had blood shed over them, were now proving totally inadequate for some very large and important items on their mission agenda, such as "the evangelization of the world."[6]

These new voluntary societies were to have profound implications for the churches. Like parishes or congregations, they were designed to bring people within hearing range of the gospel and to bring them into the church, but they did not fit into ecclesiastical systems of governance. So a new type of church organization grew up alongside old ones, and was parasitically related to them, but not under their authority. In the nineteenth century, there was an explosion of voluntary societies, as zealous evangelicals immediately saw opportunities to put these new organizational tools to work, for the reformation as well as the evangelization of their homelands.

There were other implications raised by the new voluntary mission societies. They enhanced both the opportunities to minister and the avenues to religious power and authority for laypeople, who in the old church systems had little opportunity for leadership outside of their home congregations. Now, great Christian organizations like the London Missionary Society could grow up without any say-so or trusteeship from bishops and presbyters. Before too long, another revolutionary development occurred: women organized mission societies, and women led them, too. The secret to the power and scope of these organizations was their democratic and populist appeal. They went straight to the Christian laity and pled their case. Their essential medium, which they used to great organizational benefit, was the religious magazine.[7]

By the late nineteenth century and for perhaps a hundred years following, the older churches made a major comeback in their struggle with the voluntary societies, by borrowing a model from the business world—the multifunction, comprehensive corporation. This was the age of denominational consolidation, and many formerly independent voluntary societies were absorbed into denominational organizational charts. Twentieth-century denominational and ecumenical impulses in Protestantism have been governed more than is remembered or admitted by the model of the business corporation. The formation of the World Council of Churches in 1948 was in one sense the epitome of that tendency. It consolidated and bureaucratized a variety of ecumenical and missionary movements and societies. Not incidentally, it seems, Protestantism, Incorporated, was drawing its energy from a more pragmatic and modernistic theology and sense of mission.

While mainline Protestantism was being incorporated, evangelical populists were moving full speed ahead with the older but abidingly subversive model of relying on voluntary societies to do Christian work. They were driven by the same old missionary impulses, but they began to develop fresh protests as well, expressed in the holiness, pentecostal, and fundamentalist movements. Evangelicals were becoming marginalized within the corporate-modeled Protestant denominations, and many of them made these voluntary societies their chief media for mission and ministry outside their home congregations. So the contemporary evangelical heirs of these movements are radically oriented toward parachurch agencies in their approach to ministry. They are following this two-century-old proclivity with more single-mindedness than ever. Churchly concerns about polity and sacraments are not terribly interesting to them, and they have been distrustful of what the post-fundamentalist leader Harold Ockenga once called the "managerial revolution" in churchly affairs.

One of the more frustrating features of this parachurch pattern for would-be partners from other traditions is that it is virtually impossible for them to say to the evangelicals, "take me to your leader." It is similarly difficult to gather a group of evangelical sages and activists, from a variety of sectors of their vast complex of churches and ministries, and to say, here is a truly representative gathering of evangelical leaders. Some of the greatest statesmen of the movement in recent decades, such as John Stott and Billy Graham, may be earnestly desirous of pan-Christian fellowship and partnership. Yet even they cannot presume to speak for all, and they are pointedly reminded of that all of the time. As Ronald Wells, one of my colleagues at Calvin College, once quipped in a moment of exasperation, "I want to turn in my evangelical membership card, but I don't know where to send it!"

In these several ways, then, evangelical Christianity has been a divisive, balkanizing force in modern Christianity. Agents of ecumenical dialogue and partnership in mission have some justification for feeling hesitant about reaching out to them.

Evangelical Christianity as a Unitive Force

It would be a big mistake, and deeply unfair as well, if this background briefing ended here, for there are some profoundly unitive and ecumenical features to evangelical movements and traditions. A classic case is the Pietist movement. Count Zinzendorf's Herrnhutt community, for example, readily blended Reformed, Lutheran, Czech Hussite, and even Roman Catholic people in common fellowship and mission. Later Puritans, church historian Richard Lovelace is eager to tell us, were attracted to this expression of spiritual unity and common cause in mission, particularly Cotton Mather, who struck up a warm correspondence with several Pietist theologians in Europe. The late Puritan master of pastoral theology, Richard Baxter, was fond of the saying that the Wesleys later adopted: "Unity in essentials, liberty in incidentals, and in all things, charity."[8]

The Great Awakening itself, for all of its disruption, had its unitive aspects as well. In the most fervent moments of a revival, evangelicals have tended to see Christianity configured in a vastly different way from what appears through the ordinary ecclesiastical structures. In a revival, the Spirit is no respecter of denominations, but moves where it will, and people are to respond without regard to churchly backgrounds or structures. They find unprecedented unity in their refreshed spiritual commitments and in their renewed missionary zeal. Revivals are times of liminality, as the anthropologists call it, when ordinary rules, structures, and expectations are suspended, and all things become possible to those who believe, and who are empowered and enlightened by the Spirit.[9] Revivals tend to be followed by times of creative energy as the born-again and spirit-filled start new agencies, launch new initiatives, and work with new partners.

The great American church historian Winthrop Hudson argued that the Awakening in colonial America had a unitive impact. In addition to its many disruptions and controversies, it also forged a new, pan-Protestant evangelicalism, he says, with a unitive emphasis. It helped create a new departure in ecclesiastical understanding, called denominationalism. Instead of saying, in effect, to one's neighboring churches, "We're a church, and you're a sect," now Christian leaders talked, as seldom before, about the church of Christ, "variously denominated." George Whitefield, preaching from the courthouse balcony in Philadelphia, captured the mood with a little play-acting: "Fa-

ther Abraham, whom have you in heaven? Any Episcopalians?
No! Any Presbyterians? No! Any Independents or Methodists?
No, no, no! Who have you there? We don't know those names
here. All who are here are Christians. . . . Oh, is this the case?
Then God help us to forget party names and to become Chris-
tians in deed and in truth."[10]

In a similar way, just as evangelical impulses for renewal
and revival bring both disruption and unity, so too do evangelicals' organizational and entrepreneurial tendencies. At the
same time that evangelical parachurch agencies have made a
hash out of traditional ecclesiology, they have also brought
people together across ecclesiastical boundaries. It is important
in this respect to recall that perhaps the most powerful forces
behind the formation of the World Council of Churches were
the turn-of-the-century parachurch agencies for the evangelization of students and the student movements for the evangelization of the world. Some have quipped that the World Council
was able to be established because of the "old boys' network"
of the disciples of John R. Mott. It is equally true that the Lausanne Committee for World Evangelization was made possible
because of the InterVarsity old boys' network of the disciples of
John Stott. Parachurch agencies are gifted at bringing people together in mission from a wide variety of Christian traditions.
Wheaton College, for example, where I used to teach, is a parachurch agency, not a denominational college such as Calvin
College. Wheaton today is in many ways friendlier to the more
Reformed wing of evangelicalism than to the Wesleyan and
other major persuasions, but it has nearly every Protestant persuasion represented within its faculty and staff. Episcopalians,
Lutherans, Presbyterians and Reformed, Baptists, Methodists,
Mennonites, Evangelical Free and Evangelical Covenant people, and members of the Churches of Christ, the Christian and
Missionary Alliance, the Salvation Army, the Assemblies of
God, and independent evangelical churches make common
cause in providing an evangelical higher education. In this
sense, Wheaton College is more ecumenical than the two area
councils of churches, both the exclusively evangelical one and
the mainline Protestant one.

My experience with inner-city ministry in Philadelphia brought
me into partnership with another amazing instance of local-

ized, task-oriented evangelical ecumenism. Four powerful voluntary organizations for ministry—Black Clergy, Inc., the Hispanic Clergy Association, the Korean Ministerium, and the Philadelphia Leadership Foundation—were all in close fellowship with each other. Three of the four groups shared an office suite donated by a downtown bank, and the black and Korean clergy went on a powerful reconciliation retreat together after the Los Angeles riots in 1992. Lutheran, Presbyterian, United Church of Christ, Episcopal, Assemblies of God, Church of God in Christ pastors and leaders, plus Baptists, independents, the Reformed, Methodists, and even a number of Roman Catholic parish priests and religious, too, were all working together for the sake of God's *shalom* in Philly. They were mounting campaigns against the drug dealers and for new and renovated housing, day care, and tutoring. They ran Bible clubs and job-training and drug rehabilitation centers. They founded or retooled Christian schools, and they accomplished much more as well. One of the great bonding and emboldening experiences for them all was working together for the 1992 Billy Graham campaign at Veterans Stadium.

Where was the local council of churches in all of this vital ministry? It was largely invisible and irrelevant. So were the denominations' stated bishops, district superintendents, executive presbyters, and high-steeple divines. They all were wringing their hands over their losses—of members, congregations, funds, and in their more reflective moments, their relevance. The civil rights movement, apparently, had been their last shining moment. It was quite clear to me, as a newcomer to town and as a foundation officer looking for effective partners to get things done, that the old-line ecumenists weren't on the "A team." Neither was the Catholic Church's resident cardinal, who was cold, critical, and aloof. His idea of ecumenical dialogue seemed to be telling Philly's Puerto Rican reverends that they were apostates. So who were the bishops in Philadelphia? It is no accident that in recent campaigns for federal support for faith-based agencies, Philadelphia has been held up as a shining example of what they can accomplish.

Here, then, is a new ecumenism, a local, mission-oriented variety, operating largely through congregations and the voluntary societies linking them. The "fortunate subversion," as

Walls put it, of the traditional church structures is still occur-ring, and evangelicals, despite all of their frustrating tendencies toward divisiveness, are playing essential roles on the ground, if not so much in the formal councils. We live in fragmenting times. Even in an age of global connectivity and interdepen-dence, there is a great devolution of grand alliances, of consoli-dated corporate monoliths, and even of the power and salience of nation-states. All politics is local, the late Speaker of the House of Representatives Tip O'Neill was fond of reminding us, and so, too, perhaps, is all ecumenism.

I am not quite ready to stake this position out as my claim, but I do see nonconciliar Christian partnership and fellowship growing, taking new shapes, and making a difference for the kingdom's sake, around the world, with evangelicals as key or-ganizers within these movements. Since coming back to Cal-vin College and entering the Christian Reformed Church, I have gained a greater awareness and appreciation for those who take ecclesiastical and sacramental issues very seriously. They can readily point out the damage that evangelical voluntarism has fostered. Yet I offer this alternative case to point out that much of the result of this subversion has indeed been fortu-nate. So how to reconcile these two arguments? I need a few more years to think about them, and would cherish the in-sights of those who are wiser and more learned than I in these matters.

Challenges for Evangelicals in Pan-Christian Partnership

In conclusion, I want to offer a few words of counsel for evan-gelicals. We cannot change who we are, but we should recog-nize that our strengths can also be our deficiencies, and try to address our shortcomings.

First, an evangelical theology of the church and the sacra-ments is deeply missing, and evangelicals are hurt by its lack. Ecclesiology seems boring to us, but perhaps there are ways to bring it back to life. One promising attempt is the recent work of the Croatian pentecostal theologian Miroslav Volf, of Yale University.[11]

Second, there is another dark side to the parachurch subver-

sion that we have not discussed, and it bears at least mention-
ing here. There are affinities between voluntarism and the individualistic, capitalist-consumerist values that have so much
power in American culture today. Individualism, we need to
understand, is more a modern human trait than a biblically
sanctioned one. Evangelicals are deeply lacking in the communal accountability and solidarity that the more sacramental
and confessional traditions have developed. Without a strong
sense of being a called-out people of God, with loyalties to
God's new nation rather than to ourselves and our secular nation or tribe, we may be missing vital aspects of God's word
and will for us today.

Third, evangelical isolation and estrangement from other
Christians is not good for us, and it is not good for the wider
networks of faith. We need to ponder anew what the Almighty
has been doing, in communions and cultural settings alien to
our own. There is a wideness to God's mercy that we are not
fully appreciating and a fellowship we are not enjoying, and
founts of wisdom from which we are not drinking. Some humility, curiosity, and yearning to learn from and to have fellowship with other Christians would help us greatly. It would
help others as well. As evangelicals, self-proclaimed people of
the gospel, we have our Jesus-centric, personalistic selves to
offer, for the good of other traditions.

Fourth, the "ecumene" of the century we are entering is
greater, grander, and more diverse than ever before. We may
well be seeing an evangelical, pentecostal moment in ecumenical circles. The rising demographic tide and influence of Christianity in the Global South, and the overwhelmingly evangelical and charismatic character of it, points to things to come in
formal international ecumenical circles as well as in local situations. Surely that should be one of the take-home messages
from the 1998 Lambeth Conference of Anglicans, from the
1995 African Synod of the Roman Catholic Church, and from
the recent election of a Methodist from Kenya to head the
World Council of Churches. The outlook, salient issues, and
terms of engagement will change rapidly in the coming century, and the old institutional wineskins may well not hold the
new wine.[12] So for evangelicals of the North Atlantic, are we in
the new ecumenical game or not? I have deep hope for a new

synthesis arising out of these global developments. Third World Christian leaders are shaping an agenda that will help Northern evangelicals, on the one hand, see that they cannot have the Messiah without signing up as agents of his *shalom*. They are teaching the liberal ecumenicals, on the other hand, that you cannot have a messianic social and political agenda that is divorced from the person of Jesus Christ.[13]

Therefore, despite the obstacles, frustrations, discomfort, uncertainty, and conflict that they might encounter in reaching out more broadly, I would encourage evangelical leaders to stay the course with the ecumenical dialogues and efforts at partnership in ministry that are now running. I want to encourage our Christian partners in conversation and mission to be patient, welcoming, and understanding as well. Grace has brought us to this point, and grace will show us the way home.

Part 2

Evangelicals and Fundamentalism

2

What Evangelicals Can Learn from Fundamentalists

Richard J. Mouw

On May 21, 1922, Harry Emerson Fosdick preached a sermon in the First Presbyterian Church of New York City on the topic, "Shall the Fundamentalists Win?" At the time, intense theological warfare was being waged in both Baptist and Presbyterian circles, and Fosdick's address was a major statement from the best-known liberal Protestant leader of the day.

Fosdick made it clear that he had little use for fundamentalist Christianity. But he also went out of his way to distinguish between conservative Christianity in general and fundamentalism in particular. "We should not identify the Fundamentalists with the conservatives," he warned his hearers. "All Fundamentalists are conservatives, but not all conservatives are Fundamentalists. The best conservatives can often give lessons to the liberals in true liberality of spirit, but the Fundamentalist program is essentially illiberal and intolerant."[1]

There has never been any doubt in my mind that Fosdick's description and assessment of the fundamentalism of his day contained much that was unfair. But for all of that, I have always appreciated that at least he exempted some folks who held to conservative theological views from his harsher condemnations. Indeed, for many of us who claim the "evangeli-

cal" label, distancing ourselves from fundamentalism while affirming many of the doctrines associated with fundamentalist
Christianity has been almost a full-time occupation.

I certainly have expended much energy throughout my career in preserving that sense of distance. I have done so by
telling anyone who had ears to hear a story that gives my own
personal spin to the larger narrative that has shaped the broad
evangelical movement that intentionally began to disassociate
itself from fundamentalism in the years immediately following
World War II.

Here is a brief version of the story I have often told. As the
1940s rolled around, many conservative Protestants who up to
then had been identifying themselves with fundamentalism
began to express discomfort over what they saw as three unfortunate features of the fundamentalist outlook. It was a concern
with these defects that energized the pioneers of the postwar
"neo-evangelical movement."

The first defect was *anti-intellectualism.* The fundamentalists were not very interested in seriously cultivating the life of
the mind. They tended to respond to important intellectual issues by relying on clichés, proof-texts, and clever conversation-
stoppers: "Don't give me exegesis, just give me Jesus." "Let no
man deceive you with vain philosophies." "The Bible says the
whale swallowed Jonah, and I believe it. I would also believe it
if the Bible said that Jonah swallowed the whale!"

In their efforts to correct this pattern, the neo-evangelicals
called for a new kind of scholarship, one that was faithful to
biblical orthodoxy while grappling with significant intellectual
challenges. Thus, Carl Henry called, in his 1947 book, *The Uneasy Conscience of Modern Fundamentalism,* for a new evangelical scholarly initiative that

> would develop a competent literature in every field of study,
> on every level from the grade school through the university,
> which adequately presents each subject with its implications
> from the Christian as well as non-Christian points of view. . . .
> Evangelicalism must contend for a fair hearing for the Chris-
> tian mind, among other minds, in secular education. Almost
> every philosophic viewpoint can be taught by men who hold
> these convictions—whether Platonism, Aristotelianism, Kant-
> ianism, Hegelianism, or whatever else—except that the uni-

versities seem studiously to avoid the competent presentation of the Hebrew-Christian view by those who hold it.[2]

The second defect was *otherworldliness*. This too was a feature that Carl Henry critiqued in his lament over fundamentalism's uneasy conscience. And he was joined in this by Harold John Ockenga, who observed in his introduction to Henry's *Uneasy Conscience* that "the Bible-believing Christian [has been] on the wrong side of social problems such as war, race, class, labor, liquor, imperialism, etc., [and] it is time to get over the fence to the right side."[3] The problem here was not merely one of inattention. Fundamentalists had come to understand their place in the present order of things within a theological framework that placed a high value on cultural marginalization. Specifically, their theological self-understanding—drawing on classical pietist themes and reinforcing them in many fundamentalist quarters by an espousal of dispensationalist thinking—featured a remnant ecclesiology in which the true church was seen as a cognitive minority, an apocalyptic eschatology that understood the larger culture as heading toward destruction, and an antitheticalist epistemology that insisted on a radical discontinuity between Christian and non-Christian interpretations of reality.

The third defect was a spirit of *ecclesiastical separatism*. The fundamentalists were strongly inclined to insist on strict doctrinal agreement as a necessary condition for Christian fellowship. Here too the proof-texting pattern carried the day: "Come ye out from among them and be ye separate"; "Touch not the unclean thing"; "How can two walk together unless they be agreed?" The neo-evangelicals reacted strongly against the fundamentalist penchant for splitting churches over what looked to others like minor disagreements—for example, over "pre-tribulationist" versus "post-" or "mid-tribulationist" understandings of Bible prophecy.

Beginning in the 1940s, the neo-evangelicals initiated an alternative program that embodied the new emphases they were articulating. The National Association of Evangelicals was formed to provide a more inclusive organizational context for pan-evangelical partnerships. Billy Graham promoted an intentionally non-separatist brand of "cooperative evangelism." Fuller Seminary was established with the hope that it would soon become, depending on which founding voice you were listening to, either "the Princeton of the West" or the "Cal Tech of evangelicalism." *Christianity Today* came into being as a prominent journalistic voice for the new evangelical mood. And so on.

That, then, is a short version of the story that I have told many times over the past decades. But I must confess that the story has gotten increasingly more complex in my own mind in very recent years. I have felt obligated—simply for the sake of personal integrity—regularly to add some nuances to the narrative. And it was precisely this growing sense of obligation that led me to write my book *The Smell of Sawdust*, published by Zondervan in the autumn of 2000.

Just recently I was reading a review of a book by an author who had published a kind of "tell-all" account of his relationship with his father, a well-known medical fitness expert. These comments by the reviewer leaped out at me as I read the review: "Toward the end of writing a difficult and painful memoir an author will sometimes feel a rush of shame or fear: How could I have put this on paper?" I have to admit that this comment recalled my own mood when I sent my *Sawdust* book off to the publisher. Not that I see that book as an especially "difficult and painful memoir." I actually enjoyed writing it. But it was a memoir of sorts. And I really did ask myself, as I took a last look at the finished product before handing it over to the professional editors: "How could I have put this on paper?"

Part of that reaction had to do, of course, with a sense of vulnerability about having written so much in the first person, and about youthful experiences and members of my immediate family. While I was writing the book, I found it therapeutic to go through the process of recording those memories. For the sorts of reasons I have already sketched out, many of us have worked hard over several decades to distance ourselves from fundamentalism. Now I was suggesting that we might have created too great a distance.

But I pushed ahead—and thus far have not incurred too much hostility from other evangelicals. Maybe more of us than

I thought was the case are ready for a new look at the relationship between the newer evangelicalism and the older fundamentalism. However that may be, let me at least lay out here what I think are some of the things that we ought to be taking seriously in this regard. In doing so, I must make it clear that I am not calling for a return to fundamentalism. Nor do I have any delusions that present-day fundamentalists will be happy with the sorts of positive assessments I am offering. But I do think there are significant points where we evangelicals ought to be more appreciative of fundamentalism than we have allowed ourselves to be in recent decades. I will make my points in the form of several theses that I will briefly set forth—but which I am prepared to defend at greater length if need be.

The first thesis is this: *Fundamentalism's defects are not as bad as they are sometimes made out to be.*

For one thing, the defects that I have singled out are not quite as far-reaching as I have claimed. Take anti-intellectualism, for example. It is certainly unfair to accuse fundamentalists of not being interested at all in the serious examination of ideas. As I have thought about my youthful experiences, I have had to admit that many of my later theological and philosophical interests were first nurtured by hearing fundamentalists argue with each other—at length and often with considerable precision—about infant versus adult baptism, free-will versus predestination, and even questions about a pre-tribulation rapture versus a mid- or post-tribulationist perspective.

Or take otherworldliness. Fundamentalists may not have had a strong perspective on issues of social justice, but they often had a wonderful sensitivity to certain groups of poor and marginalized people. For example, long before I ever heard of St. Francis of Assisi, or the Catholic Worker Movement, or Mother Teresa, or *Sojourners* magazine, or "a preferential option for the poor," I was regularly taken as a child to rescue-mission services, where I saw fundamentalists who devoted their lives to kneeling alongside drunks at the altar rail, to healing the wounds of unwashed bodies, and to feeding the homeless and the destitute.

And the separatistic spirit of fundamentalism. While all of the fundamentalists that I knew in my youth held to some

form of separatism, many of them were nonetheless very loving and forgiving people who genuinely cared about the spiritual well-being of people with whom they strongly disagreed.

Furthermore, even if fundamentalism's defects *were* manifested in a consistently defective way, we should not, in reject-
ing their defects, go to the opposite extreme. Anti-intellectualism may be a regrettable outlook, but so is a thoroughgoing
intellectualizing of Christianity. We can criticize otherworldliness, but this does not mean that we should immerse ourselves
in a passionate this-worldliness. Nor is an ecumenical promis-
cuity a proper alternative to rigid separatism.

In his 1995 book, *Evangelicalism and the Future of Christianity*, Alister McGrath registered many of the concerns I am
expressing here, without using the terminology that I have employed. In noticeably worried tones, McGrath urged evangelicals to continue to emphasize the experiential dimensions of
the Christian life, calling contemporary men and women into a
vital relationship with the heaven-sent Savior. In doing so he
was not downplaying the need for careful scholarship and clear
thinking. But he did insist that we can best meet that need by
keeping alive a vision of Christian wholeness "in which theologians are evangelists and evangelists theologians."[4] This is
necessary, he said, if we are to face some of the genuine challenges posed by the upward mobility that evangelicals have experienced in recent years: the movement's "sustained growth,
increasing intellectual sophistication and growing acceptance
within the churches."[5]

My second thesis is this: *Fundamentalism deserves much
credit for its organizational savvy.*

On this subject I have been helped immensely by Joel Carpenter's wonderful 1997 book, *Revive Us Again: The Reawakening of American Fundamentalism*, a study of developments
in the fundamentalist movement from 1930 through 1950. By
the end of the 1920s, the fundamentalists appeared to have lost
their battle with the modernists to gain control of the mainline
denominational seminaries and missionary agencies. Because
of this, most sophisticated observers relegated them to the
stockpile of religious history. Twenty-five years later, however,
the fundamentalist cause was very much alive and well. What

happened between 1930 and the 1950s to bring about a reversal in fundamentalism's fortunes?

Here, in brief, is Carpenter's answer. The battles against the modernists had plunged the fundamentalists into a mood of deep cultural pessimism. They came to see their role in the larger culture in "remnant" terms: they were the faithful cognitive minority who possessed inside "prophetic" information about the world's inevitable decline toward doom. The only hope for the future was the ushering in of a supernaturally initiated millennial kingdom. In the meantime, the faithful remnant had to concentrate on the work of spiritual rescue, by means of evangelizing the lost and providing spiritual nurture for the remnant.

Much of Carpenter's narrative focuses on the intricate subculture the fundamentalists constructed to implement their mission. While the secularizing elites took it for granted that "the old-time religion" was a thing of the past, the fundamentalists were building a complex system of independent organizations: youth ministries, evangelistic teams, Bible institutes, seminaries, missionary agencies, summer Bible conferences, Bible distribution societies, and so on. These organizations were actually somewhat eclectic theologically: advocates of the "Old Princeton" brand of Presbyterian Calvinism managed to cooperate in various settings with both the more "Bible prophecy"–oriented dispensational theology and the relatively atheological "get the message out"–type pragmatists. The fundamentalist subculture was surprisingly transdenominational, with participants representing the newer independent "Bible churches" as well as pockets of conservatism within the more established denominational bodies.

During the period when the fundamentalists were building this organizational infrastructure, the old-line Protestant bodies seemed content to maintain the more traditional denominational patterns. Their efforts at creating new interdenominational networks focused primarily on leadership-oriented "council of churches" entities, in contrast to the fundamentalists' less "official" grassroots networks.

In all of this, Carpenter argues, the liberals were oblivious to the fact that they were being outflanked by the theological opponents whom they thought they had defeated in the earlier battles. As Carpenter puts it, although the process was not very visible for several decades, the fundamentalists were helping to effect "a major shift among the basic institutional carriers of American religious life." The results are quite obvious today: the old-line "denominations have been losing members, income, and influence while special-purpose, non-denominational religious agencies have grown, multiplied, and taken on increasing importance in shaping and carrying people's religious identity." Carpenter underscores the irony in this situation. They had been forced by the Protestant establishment to move to the margins, and, in order to survive, the fundamentalists guaranteed their own survival by initiating "a trend that has led to the weakening of the most central and powerful corporate expressions of American religion."[6]

A third thesis: *Fundamentalism contributed much to the strength of the broader evangelical movement.*

In a sense, this is obvious from what I have just outlined. Many of the organizations built by fundamentalists—Young Life, Youth for Christ, Biola University, and the like—are now more broadly evangelical, but they have built on strong fundamentalist organizational foundations. Even Fuller Seminary, well known for being as "neo" as a neo-evangelical seminary can get, had its origins in the ministry of the fundamentalist evangelist Charles E. Fuller, one of the great pioneers in religious broadcasting.

The positive legacy also extends, however, directly into the spiritual realm. Here, too, Carpenter is very helpful. As he develops his analysis, Carpenter is candid about his own affection for fundamentalism. He looks at the movement from the perspective of an evangelical who wants to honor the movement's strengths while exploring its weaknesses. In making his case he is not afraid to aim a few critical arrows at his fellow "post-fundamentalist" evangelicals. Take the case of Edward John Carnell, a leader among that group of "new evangelicals" in the 1950s who chided their fundamentalist forebears for the sorts of defects I have already discussed. Carnell (who was one of my predecessors in the presidency of Fuller Theological Seminary) labeled fundamentalism "orthodoxy gone cultic,"

and spoke disparagingly of the pettiness of many of the movement's attitudes and legalisms.[7]

But, as Carpenter shows, there is a certain measure of naïveté
embodied in these criticisms. All religious movements that are
trying to accomplish something important are necessarily "cultic." They need to "devise 'mores and symbols' to live by," says
Carpenter, "and these, by their very nature as human fabrica-
tions, reflect the circumstances of their makers." Furthermore,
Carnell and his colleagues failed to acknowledge that in their
efforts to improve on what the fundamentalists had done, they
were making use of the very subculture that they were attempt-
ing to alter. "Fundamentalism was often intellectually lame,
provincial, petty, mean-spirited, stultifying and manipulative,
but it could be enabling and energizing as well, and by the 1940s
it had produced a restive and visionary younger generation."[8]

As I read Carpenter's book, I realized that while I had been
one of the people who had long been detailing the ways in
which fundamentalism could be "intellectually lame, provincial, petty, mean-spirited, stultifying and manipulative," I had
not been very honest about the ways it could also be "enabling
and energizing." This acknowledgment had much to do with
motivating me to write *The Smell of Sawdust.*

A fourth thesis: *We still have much to learn from fundamentalism's understanding of its relationship to the larger
culture.*

I began my career as an evangelical activist, expending much
energy in calling evangelicals to get more involved in working
for the cause of the kingdom in the public arena. I must confess, however, that there have been many times in recent years
when, given the ways in which many newly active evangelicals have behaved in the public sphere, I have secretly longed
for the earlier days when we all sang "This world is not my
home, I'm just a-passing through," rather than "Shine, Jesus,
shine, fill this land with the Father's glory."

As I mentioned earlier, the older fundamentalism had an outlook that was characterized by these three theological strands: a
remnant ecclesiology, apocalyptic eschatology, and an antitheticalist epistemology. Today many evangelicals come danger-
ously close to adopting a triumphalist "church growth" ecclesi-

ology, a functional post-millenialist eschatology, and a "moral majority" epistemology. In my better moments, of course, I know that the appropriate response about all of this is one of ambivalence. The answer is not to retreat again into a separatist mode, but to move more cautiously into the public arena while submitting to the discipline of careful evangelical reflection. But this does mean that we need to think much more than we have been inclined to in recent years about the positive lessons to be learned from the times of our past marginalization.

Actually, there is some help to be gained for this reflective task by thinking critically about the views being put forth these days by some non-evangelical scholars.[9] Many of our own past evangelical attitudes and moods have been taken up with a vengeance by ethicists in other segments of the Christian community. It is not difficult to find, for example, strong hints in the direction of the older remnant-apocalyptic-antithetical motifs in the writings of Stanley Hauerwas, who has been very vocal in his insistence that Christian ethics must be grounded in the practices of a highly particularized Christian community that sees its moral discourse as radically discontinuous with that of the larger culture.

While evangelicals should not uncritically embrace these current blends of remnant ecclesiology, apocalyptic eschatology, and antitheticalist epistemology, neither should we simply dismiss them out of hand. Again, this seems to me to be an important time to go back over the steps that took us from the excesses of the older fundamentalism to the excesses of much recent evangelical social activism.

A final thesis: *There is some wisdom in fundamentalism's very central emphasis on bringing people to a personal relationship to Christ.*

Bill Hybels has been reflecting out loud recently about what he sees as the mistakes he and his staff have made in recent years at Willow Creek Church by setting priorities in such a way that evangelism has a kind of equal standing with other important goals. We have a special tendency, he argues, to downplay evangelism, so that when we assign it equal value with other areas of Christian mission, we actually end up letting it slip a bit down the scale of priorities. Only when we emphasize evangelism above all else, Hybels now insists, will it receive its due as *one* of the important functions of the church.

There is much to be said for the point Hybels is making. Back in the 1970s, when I and other evangelical social activists were making the case for what I called, in the title of my first book, "political evangelism," I regularly complained about what I saw as too strong an emphasis on personal evangelism, at the expense of such things as addressing the physical needs of the poor and working in the political arena. One of the choruses from my youth that I often cited as an example of a fundamentalist distortion of the Christian life had this refrain: "Saved, saved to tell others." We aren't simply saved to tell others, I would insist. We are saved to participate in a community that shows forth the will of God for all dimensions of human life. We are saved to *be* something: disciples who are living reconciled lives and are serving as agents of reconciliation. Evangelism is one important part of the picture—but it is not the whole picture.

I still believe that is basically correct. But I worry about the unintended effects of that way of putting it. We cannot simply put evangelism on a longer "to do" list and hope that it will be carried out with the appropriate passion by the Christian community.

But there is a more profound point that I want to make about what I learned from fundamentalists about a personal relationship with Jesus Christ. For me the most important moments that I spent on the sawdust trail were during the "altar call." "Every head bowed, every eye closed," the evangelist would intone. "No one looking around, please." And then we would be asked to look into our hearts. Those who did not yet know the Lord were urged to accept him right then. But the rest of us were also challenged to look into our hearts anew and think honestly about our relationship to the Lord. The hymns that reinforced that exercise in self-examination have been an extremely important component of my own spiritual formation. "Is your all on the altar of sacrifice laid?" "I surrender all." "Just as I am, without one plea, but that thy blood was shed for me." "Jesus paid it all, all to him I owe."

I miss those hymns today. I even miss the ones that directly addressed sinners who were still wandering outside the fold. For all of the harshness and rigidity of much of fundamentalism, in those moments we were ushered into the presence of a gentle Savior who was pleading with the lost to come to the place of safety. "Softly and tenderly, Jesus is calling, calling, 'O sinner, come home.'"

Those were occasions for me when I stood—in ways that I have never quite experienced elsewhere—face to face with eternity. Whatever else the sawdust trail meant to me—not all of it positive—it became for me in those moments a sacred space of the sort that I have not been able to find with the same starkness in other Christian regions.

I know that I can never simply go back to the sawdust trail that I once knew. It would be wrong even to make the attempt. But I do yearn, and not only for myself but for the larger evangelical movement, for a "second naïveté," a new experience—albeit a post-anti-intellectual and post-otherworldly and post-separatist experience—of the sense of God's presence that I once knew on the sawdust trail.

In my book I explain my recent discovery of how the sawdust-trail imagery came to be used by folks in the revivalist tradition. In the lumber camps of the Northwest, when a lumberjack got lost in the woods, he would search for traces of sawdust, and follow the trail of sawdust back to the place of safety. Early in the twentieth century, evangelists picked up on this theme, calling wandering sinners to walk the sawdust trail until they arrived at their spiritual home.

We are gathered in a time of crisis, when many of our fellow human beings in North America have realized that what they thought were their protective fortresses are in fact quite vulnerable to destruction and utter desolation. This is an important moment for all of us to think about how we can effectively invite sinners to come home, to find their security in the only safe place in the university—under the shadow of the Almighty at the foot of Calvary's cross. There are significant lessons to be learned in this regard from those folks whom many of us have known on the sawdust trail.

3

What's That You Smell?

A FUNDAMENTALIST RESPONSE TO *THE SMELL OF SAWDUST*

Kevin T. Bauder

Richard Mouw has written *The Smell of Sawdust* with good humor and transparency. I join many other fundamentalists in expressing appreciation for his book. Of course, this does not mean that I shall have nothing to say about it, but I hope my response can be as measured and thoughtful as Dr. Mouw's original.

Since the publication of George Marsden's *Fundamentalism and American Culture* in 1980, discussions about American fundamentalism have proliferated. Those of us who still call ourselves fundamentalists appreciate the attention, and we acknowledge our indebtedness not only to Marsden, but also to such evangelical scholars as Mark Noll, D. G. Hart, Nathan Hatch, and Joel Carpenter. Valuable as their contributions are, however, we fundamentalists often walk away from their writings with the impression that we have seen our reflection in a convex mirror. The features are certainly recognizable, but at least some of the proportions seem wrong. We feel that we have been ever so slightly stereotyped. Frankly, I experienced the same sensation after reading President Mouw's book.

The distortion occurs, I think, not out of any ill will or care-

lessness, but from the unavoidable deficiency of not having jos-
tled one's own way through the corridors of fundamentalism.
Outsiders—even those who grew up in fundamentalism—seem
to see fundamentalism as a rather flat movement in which fundamentalists are similar in most important respects. I suggest,
however, that fundamentalism is not a single movement, but a
collection of distinct movements that are shaped by competing
influences. Some forms of fundamentalism display surprising
twists and contours.

The failure to distinguish the separate species of fundamentalists is often aggravated by the tendency to define fundamentalism in terms of its accoutrements and unintended effects instead of its essence. The result is the same as if one were to
define a hammer as a device for producing blisters on the hand.
This result occurs whenever fundamentalism is treated *primarily* in terms of dispensationalism, pre-millennialism, common-
sense realism, populism, revivalism, or anti-intellectualism. I
do not for a moment deny that many fundamentalists are characterized by each of these categories. I concede that such categories are useful in doing social and theological analyses of the
various movements within fundamentalism. None of them,
however, really gets to the heart of fundamentalism. For example, there have always been fundamentalists who are not dis-
pensationalists, and there are non-fundamentalists who are.

If you ask me whether I am a fundamentalist, my answer
will depend upon which fundamentalism you mean. Of the
various species of fundamentalism, I could not possibly identify with more than one, and I am even uncomfortable with
some of the things that happen there. Having expressed this
ambivalence about fundamentalist movements, however, I
must hasten to add that the term *fundamentalism* does not
merely denote the movements, or even the movement as a
whole. Fundamentalism is not primarily a social phenomenon,
but an *idea*. And I am much more concerned with the *idea* of
fundamentalism than I am with the fundamentalist movement
or movements. In terms of the idea, I am unabashedly a fundamentalist. I believe fundamentalism was and is a great idea, an
idea that is thoroughly in keeping with the best of Christian
thought as it has been mediated through the Reformation.

To begin, fundamentalism has inherited the Reformation distinction between the invisible and the visible church.[1] In mainstream Protestant ecclesiology, the invisible church is the communion of the saints and the body of Christ. The Holy Spirit unites to this body as many as place their trust in Christ as Savior, joining them organically to Christ and to one another. The invisible church, then, is the church of those who possess saving faith in Christ. It is called the *invisible* church because its essential, constituting elements are not available for immediate inspection. A person's heart cannot be inspected for the presence of faith, nor can that person's union with Christ be directly examined. In Protestant thought, the invisible church is the true church, the church to which biblical promises, prerogatives, and predicates apply. It alone is unequivocally one, holy, catholic, and apostolic.[2]

If the invisible church is the body of those who *possess* true, saving faith in Jesus Christ, the visible church is the company of those who *profess* true faith. The visible church is the empirical church. Because profession does not necessarily equal possession, however, the visible church at its best only approximates the true church. Biblical promises, prerogatives, and predicates apply to it only in a relative sense.[3]

Because we cannot infallibly judge who possesses true faith, we cannot say with certainty who is in the true, invisible church. A profession of faith, however, is an empirical thing. It can be heard and evaluated. The genius of Protestant ecclesiology is to recognize only those who profess true faith as members of the visible church.[4]

When one professes faith, one claims to believe the gospel and to receive Jesus Christ as Savior. At first glance, it might appear that this profession ought to be evaluated purely on experiential grounds, perhaps by its fervency. Fervency alone, however, does not speak to the content of one's faith. People may experience a fervent trust in and devotion to the wrong things. So we must ask content questions, such as, When you claim to believe in Jesus, do you mean the Jesus of Arius or of Athanasius?

Such questions are irrecusably doctrinal. They imply a second insight that fundamentalists have inherited from the Reformation. This insight is that the gospel, and therefore the Christian faith, includes a doctrinal component. This does not mean that fundamentalists reduce Christianity to doctrine alone—far from it. With historic Protestants, they recognize that the Christian faith also includes both practical duties and ordinate affections. Fundamentalists are aware that orthopraxy and orthopathy stand alongside of orthodoxy as essential elements of the Christian faith.[5] Still, even though fundamentalists see Christianity as more than doctrinal, they never see it as less.

None of this means that all doctrines are equally important. Most fundamentalists recognize several levels of importance between doctrines, but one level is especially significant for this discussion. All fundamentalists insist that certain doctrines are so important as to enter into the definition of Christianity. These doctrines are traditionally known as *essential* or *fundamental* doctrines.[6]

Fundamentalists did not invent the idea of fundamental doctrines. They inherited it. The distinction between fundamental (essential, capital, cardinal, or chief) doctrines (articles, heads) and nonfundamental doctrines is found in the Lutheran, Calvinist, and Arminian branches of Protestantism. This distinction was affirmed by the Reformers themselves, as well as by the Protestant scholastics.[7]

In classical Protestantism, the fundamentals are doctrines upon which the gospel itself depends. This does not mean that people need to have a clear and distinct knowledge of every fundamental in order to be converted. A. A. Hodge drew an important distinction: "A fundamental doctrine . . . is either one which every soul must apprehend more or less clearly in order to be saved, or one which, when known, is so clearly involved with those the knowledge and belief of which is essential to salvation, that the one cannot be rejected while the other is really believed."[8] In both cases, the denial of a fundamental doctrine implies a denial of the gospel itself. According to traditional Protestantism, any person who denies a fundamental doctrine is implicitly denying the gospel.

Since the visible church is the body of those who profess faith, those who deny the gospel must not be reckoned as part of the visible church. This is easy to see in the case of a Saracen or a Hindu, but Protestants also apply this principle to people who deny fundamental doctrines while naming the name of Christ. We are not entitled to judge the salvation of such individuals, for we cannot observe their hearts. We are, however, obligated to evaluate their professions of faith for their consistency with the gospel. We cannot say with certainty whether they are members of the invisible church, but we can know whether they ought to be reckoned in the company of the visible church.

In historic Protestantism, the fundamentals were especially important for distinguishing true churches of Jesus Christ from spurious ones. According to Calvin, doctrine was a sine qua non for the existence of Christianity. This observation played directly into his discussion of how to distinguish a true church from a counterfeit one.[9] The idea, however, is not merely a Calvinistic idea. Substantially the same argument shows up in the disputations of Arminius.[10]

Just as individuals who deny fundamental doctrines of the gospel cannot be reckoned as Christians, so churches that deny fundamental doctrines of the gospel cannot rightly be regarded as true Christian churches. Luther put it this way: "Now the certain mark of the Christian congregation is the preaching of the Gospel in its purity. . . . [W]here the Gospel is not preached and the doctrines of men hold sway, there can be no Christians but only heathens, no matter how great their numbers or how saintly and good their lives." Churches that do not preach the gospel in purity are engaging in "purely human affairs under cover of the name of a Christian congregation."[11] For Luther, the test of a true church, like the test of a true Christian, was first of all doctrinal.

This consideration is especially important for those who believe that Christians must unite with a particular church. Most Protestant ecclesiologies stress that membership in a particular church is not optional.[12] Franz Pieper, a conservative Lutheran theologian, argued that the local church is a divine institution from which individual Christians have no authority to exempt themselves.[13] John Gerstner represented the Presbyterian and Reformed tradition when he wrote, "We must belong to a church if at all possible. That is our duty. We must therefore not separate from a church unless necessary. Not to join a church is a sin of omission; to separate unnecessarily from a church is a sin of commission."[14] Expressing an Arminian point of view, John Miley dedicated an entire page of his *Systematic Theology* to listing reasons for thinking that church membership is a duty.[15] Classical Protestants in general have taken church membership very seriously.

If church membership is obligatory, then the existence of spurious churches poses a special problem. If a person is a member of a false church, it follows that that person is not a member of a true church. Not to be a member of a true church, however, violates a Christian duty. This was the insight that J. Gresham Machen grasped when thinking about his own church, the councils of which he believed to be dominated by modernism. "Such a body is hardly what the Bible means by a church at all. The Bible commands Christian people to be members of a true church, even though it be an imperfect one. It represents the nurture provided by such a true church as a necessity, not a luxury, in the Christian life. There must therefore be a separation. . . ."[16] Bluntly, people who prefer membership in false churches to membership in true ones are guilty of grave disobedience.

Machen preferred to reform his church by purging the modernists from its leadership. If reformation proved impossible, however, he was quite prepared to provoke a separation. Accused of being schismatic, Machen replied that not every separation is a schism. "All Protestants have made themselves party to a separation from an existing church organization." Therefore, some separations are not only permissible, but are "an inescapable and very solemn Christian duty." Machen summarized: "Here, then, is the principle of the thing—it is schism to leave a church if that church is true to the Bible, but it is not schism if that church is not true to the Bible. In the latter case, far from its being schism to separate from the church in question, it is schism to remain in it, since to remain in it means to disobey the Word of God and to separate oneself from the true Church of Jesus Christ."[17]

In these lines, Machen captured the core of the fundamentalist idea: the belief that Christian unity and fellowship are possible only with other Christians. This has to be the case, for unity is a function of that which unites, and fellowship is a function of that which is held in common. Within the *visible* church, what is held in common is the *profession* of the gospel, and the profession of the gospel can always be evaluated by the test of fundamental doctrines. To put it concisely, fundamentalists insist that it is always wrong for Christians to pretend that they can enjoy Christian unity and fellowship with those who deny fundamental doctrines, for such persons really deny the gospel itself.

In other words, what we are now discussing is separatism. Separatism is the heart of fundamentalism. Whatever else they may quarrel about, all fundamentalists agree that no Christian fellowship or union is possible with those who deny the gospel by denying fundamental doctrines. This separatism does not arise (as has sometimes been suggested) from dispensationalism, but from a thoroughly Protestant way of looking at the visible church.[18]

For fundamentalists, this works out in three ways. First, they insist upon purging from their churches and institutions all spokespersons who deny the gospel.[19] Second, they refuse Christian cooperation and fellowship with any organization or movement that supports the denial of the gospel.[20] Third, they refuse to grant recognition as Christians to, or engage in any activity that would imply Christian commonality with, teachers or other leaders who deny the gospel.

Most fundamentalists love the church of Jesus Christ. They value church unity and Christian fellowship. But they are convinced that those who love the Lord Jesus cannot extend Christian unity, fellowship, and cooperation to people who deny the gospel. To do so is something akin to ecclesiastical treason. Fundamentalist thought is dominated by a churchly emphasis. Something is supposed to transpire between people who are in the church that cannot transpire between people who are outside of it. They believe it is wrong to pretend to do churchly things with people whose profession places them outside of the church.

The New Evangelicalism, birthed at Fuller Theological Sem-

inary, explicitly rejected separatism. After two decades of ecclesiastical conflict, the New Evangelicals succeeded in captur-
ing the leadership of mainstream American evangelicalism. I
do not wish to revisit that struggle here.[21] I would like to suggest, however, that the rejection of separatism has ushered certain undesirable consequences into American evangelicalism.

First came a tendency to minimize doctrine as an essential
element of the gospel, replacing it with religious experience.
That is why Carnell could write, "I suffered a rude shock
when, in the course of graduate studies, I discovered a few
modernists who gave more convincing evidence of devotion to
Christ . . . than some who were celebrated for their piety in
fundamentalism. From experiences of this kind I was forced to
conclude that a person may be a true Christian, and yet have a
long way to go in the organization of his theological convictions."[22] Carnell did admit that "modernism is a system which
is contrary to the truth and should be resisted with every legitimate weapon," but he also argued that many modernists "believe a lot more in their hearts than they will admit into their
theology."[23] Since these people give evidence of evangelical repentance, argued Carnell, they should not be denied Christian
fellowship.

If Carnell only meant that some people receive truths in
their hearts that they deny in their speculative systems, most
of us would agree. But Carnell clearly meant more than that.
What Carnell wanted to do was to extend some form of Christian recognition to people who were denying the gospel. For
Carnell, fundamental doctrines could not play a definitive role
in the gospel.

Second, having minimized the role of doctrine in defining
the gospel, evangelicals became uncertain about which doctrines qualified as fundamental. This was the focus of the inerrancy debates of the 1970s and 1980s. Those debates were
much more than just political skirmishes over the boundaries
of evangelicalism. They were about the nature of biblical authority, and that problem is surely fundamental to the gospel.
At present, there is little consensus within American evangelicalism over just how much and what manner of biblical authority is fundamental to the gospel. This uncertainty also ex-

tends to other areas of fundamental doctrine. Open theism raises crucial issues about the nature of God, while the discussions among Evangelicals and Catholics Together have forced evangelicals to ask whether justification through imputed righteousness is essential to the gospel.

This brings up a third consequence that has followed the rejection of separatism. Given the present deemphasis upon doctrine, evangelicals can no longer say exactly who they are. Attempts to define evangelicalism abound, and the lack of unanimity among those definitions is notable. The Evangelical Theological Society has devoted several sessions to the problem. I suggest that this confusion is unavoidable. By its very name, evangelicalism is supposed to be tied to an evangel. If the evangel cannot be defined (an irreducibly doctrinal exercise), then evangelicals are forced to define themselves by their relationship to they know not what.

The problem, however, is even worse than that. Not only have evangelicals lost a sense of who *they* are, many of them are no longer even sure what a *Christian* is. Richard J. Mouw betrays this uncertainty in his chapter on "Understanding Sister Helen's Tears."[24] We might ask two questions about his now-deceased Romanist teacher. First, we might ask, Is she in heaven? The only correct answer to that question is that none of us is qualified to judge. Her faith and union with Christ (if they existed) were not available for public inspection. Even the presence of apparent piety and virtue is ambiguous if it is not accompanied by a profession of the gospel. But then we might ask, Would her system of doctrine lead her to heaven? Here we can answer with greater certainty. The Roman Catholic Church has not made a secret of its understanding of salvation. The way of salvation (the gospel) is also clearly revealed in Scripture. When we compare the two, we should be able to say without hesitation that, understood on its own terms and applied with consistency, the Romanist system does not save the soul.[25] The question is not (as President Mouw seems to suggest) how we present the gospel or whether we appeal for a decision. The question is about the actual content of the gospel itself, of what the gospel *is*.[26]

The current attitude toward Romanism is only one illustration of the inability of evangelicals to decide who should be recognized as a Christian. This inability was manifested as early as Carnell's speculation (noted earlier) that some modernists might be true Christians. Sometimes this inability can take startling forms. I was present at a Catholic-evangelical dialogue in which an evangelical theologian distributed copies of the National Association of Evangelicals' statement of faith, then asked if any of the Catholics who were present could deny any of it. Given its vagueness, of course they could not.[27] At that point, the evangelical explicitly invited the Roman Catholic Church to seek membership in the National Association of Evangelicals. The Catholic theologians were profoundly uncomfortable with that kind of doctrinal imprecision. They knew that the core of both systems was at stake, and they were not willing to assume that the systems were compatible simply because of superficial similarities in wording. A second evangelical theologian introduced the distinction between imputed righteousness and imparted righteousness, and the conversation snapped into focus. "Ah, yes!" said one of the Romanist theologians. "We *knew* that was what you *really* meant. And that is what we do not accept!"

I appreciate the candor of that Romanist priest, but I wonder whether he was not mistaken about one thing. I wonder whether the first evangelical really *did* grasp the centrality of the notion that justification comes only through the imputation of the alien righteousness of Christ. Indeed, I wonder how many of today's evangelicals would be willing to distinguish a Christian from an anti-Christian system upon the basis of such a doctrine.

When you lose the ability to define the evangel, you lose the ability to define evangelicalism. More than that, you lose the ability to define Christianity. I do not mean to be impertinent, but I must ask: If you can no longer define Christianity, and if you no longer know what evangelicalism is, then how can you assert that evangelicalism is still Christian?

What is the alternative? First, one must recognize the centrality of the gospel to Christian faith. Second, one must remember the importance of fundamental doctrines in defining the gospel. Third, one must apply the fundamental doctrines as a sine qua non for the veracity of professions of the gospel.

Fourth, one must not pretend that he can enjoy Christian unity, fellowship, communion, or cooperation with people whose professions deny the gospel and place them outside of the Christian faith and the visible church. If one remembers these principles and lives by them, he will not be an ecclesiological innovator. Rather, he will be implementing the first principles of the historic ecclesiologies of Protestantism. Disconcerting as it may seem, one will also have taken a first giant step toward becoming a fundamentalist.[28]

Part 3

EVANGELICALS
AND PENTECOSTALISM

4

The Azusa Street Revival Revisited

George D. McKinney

For pentecostal Christians, the sawdust trail leads to a broken-down shanty, a former livery stable, in a depressed neighborhood in the city of Los Angeles, where the Azusa Street Revival broke out.

The Legacy of Azusa

I'm a third-generation Pentecostal, Holiness member. My grandparents and my parents were saved about ten years after the Azusa revival. During that period there was a wave of anti-intellectualism, and there were many who were certain that Jesus would return most any day. One day my older siblings came home and informed my father, who had only a third-grade education, that our pastor had told us "that Jesus is coming real soon, therefore we don't need to go to school anymore." My father looked at his children and said, "Yes, you're going back to school tomorrow and if Jesus comes, he's going to find you at school."

I had the privilege of growing up in a home where we heard our parents and grandparents talk about the Azusa revival. The revival started as a concerned group of women gathered in a home in Los Angeles. The prayer meeting had grown and began to touch so many lives that they moved from the home to an address on Bonnie Brae Street. The fervency of the prayer and the manifestations of a strong visitation of God began to attract people from all over Los Angeles. Day after day, it was reported that there was such a crowd of worshipers and spectators that the city fathers took note. One morning during the exuberance of praise and shouting, the porch collapsed. There was more commotion. Following that experience, the revival soon moved to 312 Azusa Street, which had once been a Methodist church, but had been more recently converted into a livery stable. It was there that the women recognized that they needed help in the revival, and they sent for W. J. Seymour, a preacher from Houston. He came at their invitation and joined with them in prayer until there was an outpouring that was felt around the world.

I was privileged to be acquainted with some of the men who were involved directly in that great revival. I attended my first holy convocation at Mason Temple in Memphis in 1946. I shall never forget the powerful sermon that was preached by Bishop Charles Harrison Mason from Philippians 2:12–13. I can see and hear him now, *"Work out your salvation with fear and trembling, for it is God that worketh in you both to will and to do what pleases him."*

My parents did not have the advantage of health insurance and, when needed, of hospitalization. They were the parents of fourteen children. I was the ninth of the fourteen. Every time Mama would get pregnant she would write to Bishop Mason and inform him, "I'm pregnant, pray that the baby will come and be healthy and well." We were not born in hospitals. There was a midwife, Capitola Bennett, who delivered us. The cost was five dollars each. Bishop Mason prayed and the children came, and we were healthy and we were blessed by God.

It was Bishop Mason who founded the Church of God in Christ, in 1897, as a Holiness Church. But in 1906, Bishop Mason along with C. P. Jones, D. J. Young, and others left the South for Los Angeles to discover what was happening as the revival fires burned.

It was a great privilege to know Bishop C. H. Mason, a man small in stature, a humble man, who traveled this nation establishing churches. He was a contemporary of Father Divine,

Sweet Daddy Grace, and Prophet Jones. The Church of God in Christ had less than a million members when Bishop Mason died in 1961. Today, there are more than five million. When Father Divine, Daddy Grace, and Prophet Jones died, their movements generally died with them.

It was also my privilege to meet and fellowship with another person who received the baptism of the Holy Ghost at Azusa in 1907. He was Bishop Mack E. Jonas. Bishop Jonas was a colorful character remembered for his fiery preaching. He was interviewed by Leonard Lovett. That interview is included and reported in Vinson Synan's book, *Aspects of Pentecostal and Charismatic Origins.*[1] Jonas became the bishop of the Church of God in Christ in Ohio. He died in 1973. After moving to California in 1959, I had a chance to get acquainted with other pioneers who were present at the Azusa revival, including a colorful evangelist named Elder Kayhee and a pastor in Los Angeles, Lawrence Catley, who preached at my own church, St. Stephen's, a few months before his death.

I did not have the privilege of meeting other principal participants in the revival, but several of these principals must be noted here. Charles F. Parham was the founder of the Apostolic Faith movement in Topeka, Kansas. He also founded the Bethel Bible School in 1900. He was a former Methodist pastor. Parham popularized the doctrine that speaking in tongues is the initial evidence of being baptized in the Holy Spirit. W. J. Seymour was a student of Parham's. This relationship was strained after Parham visited Seymour in 1907 at Azusa, where Parham objected to the predominant African influence in the worship. He also objected to the fact that there was what he termed race-mixing in the worship and in the fellowship. Parham for some reason was never able to shake the cultural influence of racism. He was a strong supporter of the Klan and had difficulty accepting what God was doing in Azusa to remove the color barrier.

W. J. Seymour was born in 1870 in Centerville, Louisiana, the son of a slave. He moved to Houston, where he became acquainted with the pentecostal teachings and enrolled in Parham's school. Because of segregation, however, he was not allowed to sit in the classroom with the white students. He had to sit outside the window or in the hallway and listen as best as he could. But he was hungry for God, and he endured that humiliation and sought the Word and the living God. From Houston he was called to Los Angeles to join those praying women who sought a deeper spiritual life. When he went to Los Angeles, he had not yet received the baptism of the Holy Spirit with the evidence of speaking in tongues. Yet he believed that the blessing was promised to him, so he continued to pray and to seek until he received that blessing in 1906.

Charles Price Jones, another principal participant, born in 1865, was a great poet, songwriter, and gospel preacher. He had a wonderful experience with God, but he did not believe that speaking in tongues was the initial evidence of being filled with the Spirit of God. He and C. H. Mason disagreed about this doctrine. This was the basis of the conflict between Jones and Mason. They decided to go their separate ways, and this conflict resulted in the separation and formation of the Church of Christ Holiness in 1907.

The Spiritual Climate before Azusa

I turn now to the spiritual climate and attitudes that prevailed before the Azusa revival. There were still tremendous influences from the Welsh revival under Evan Roberts. There had been outpourings of the Holy Spirit in various parts of the world. In Los Angeles, a group of women gathered to pray and to seek God. They were gathering in prayer, first, because there was a deep hunger for God. They wanted God's will. They wanted to see the manifestations of God's power and of God's presence. Second, these women sought God in prayer daily because there was a deep dissatisfaction with the spiritual status quo. They were tired of religion. They longed for a living relationship with God. The conditions in the church, characterized by worldliness and carnality, disturbed them deeply. They wanted something more. Further, these praying women had a desire for intimacy with God. They were captured by a sense of holy expectation. They saw in the Book of Acts a promise that God would send a season of refreshing from his presence. They believed that God would keep that promise. Prior to these praying women meeting in Los Angeles, Brother Parham had received the gift of the Holy Spirit in Topeka, Kansas. Several others had received this experience, and Parham's Bible schools in Topeka and in Houston were beginning to influence and touch the lives of many people. There was an atmosphere of expectation. There was deep dissatisfaction. There was also a hunger for God.

Something else happened prior to the outpouring. Those who gathered in Topeka, Houston, and Los Angeles repented for sins and spiritual coldness. There was daily study of the Scriptures. There was *prayer, prayer,* and *more prayer.* The Scriptures that seemed to inform and motivate and inspire included Joel 2:28, "In the last days I will pour out my spirit upon all flesh." Also, these prayer warriors saw in the Book of Acts the pattern for the local fellowship. They believed the promise was for all believers and that miracles, signs, and wonders were evidence of revival. They rejected racism, claiming that Peter's sermon in Acts 10:34–43 settled the issue. Peter declares, "I perceive that God is no respecter of person. Out of every nation he that fears God and works righteousness is acceptable with him." They were captured by the expression in verse 44. The Holy Ghost fell on the Gentiles from the laying on of hands. They were moved by the experience recorded in Acts 19, in which the disciples go to Ephesus and find believers who had not yet heard or received the baptism of the Holy Spirit. Another Scripture that seemed to have opened their minds and spirits was Hebrews 12:14, "Follow peace with all men and holiness without which no man shall see the Lord." Then there was the clear word of instruction from Jesus in Mark 16:15–18, a word that gave them clear direction regarding evangelism, "Go ye into all the world . . ." This word assured them of the believer's authority in the faith and also of God's promise to demonstrate his power. "Ye shall lay hand upon the sick and cast out demons, and if you drink any deadly thing it will not harm you."

Vinson Synan states, "The Azusa Street Revival is commonly regarded as the beginning of the modern Pentecostal movement."[2] Although many persons had spoken in tongues before, this practice of speaking in tongues at Azusa came to the attention of the world. The revival served as the catalyst for the formation of scores of pentecostal denominations. Directly or indirectly, practically all pentecostal groups in existence today can be traced to the Azusa Missions. Synan further states "that Parham laid the . . . doctrinal foundation of the movement while Seymour served as the catalytic agent for its popularization." The early pentecostal movement was neither black nor white, but interracial. It was conducted by Seymour on the basis of complete *racial* and *sexual* equality. In this atmosphere, there emerged a pentecostal vision of unity predicated on a *common life in the Spirit, characterized by a common life of holiness* and *entire sanctification* drawn from the Wesleyan doctrines and teachings.

Frank Bartleman, who was present at Azusa, states in *Azusa Street* that "Brother Seymour was recognized as the nominal leader for the group, but we had no Pope. There was no hierarchy, we were brethren. We had no human program. The Lord himself was leading. No subjects of sermons were announced ahead of time, and no special speakers for such an hour."[3] As a matter of fact, it is said that Brother Seymour would sit with his head in a shoebox praying during the service. When the Spirit would move upon him, he would look up, hand the Bible to one of the men, and say, "Now you preach." No one knew what might be coming, what God would do. Bartleman writes, "We only recognized God. All were equal."

Not everyone understood or supported this revival. A front-page story from the *Los Angeles Times*, dated April 18, 1906, reads:

> A new sect of fanatics, breaking loose in a tumbled down shack at 312 Azusa. These devotees are of the weird doctrine practice, the most fanatical rites, preach the wildest theories and work themselves into a state of mad excitement in their peculiar zeal.

This kind of publicity only served to advertise the meeting and increase the interest and attendance. Many who came experienced salvation, the baptism of the Holy Ghost, and miraculous healings. According to Bartleman and other reporters, the liberating power of the Holy Spirit was manifested. Some were set free. Sinners were born again. The economically and socially oppressed were set free. Racists were set free. Women

were set free. The liberating power of God's presence manifested itself in the gathering of people from all races and all ethnic groups, from the Los Angeles area and from around the
world.

The Worship at Azusa

Now a word about the worship at Azusa. It was holy disorder,
spontaneous and unstructured. At first there were no instru-
ments, no hymnals. The participants sang as the Spirit gave
them a song. Songs were unrehearsed, but they were beautiful.
Some of the major songs that they borrowed from the sawdust
trail included words like, "The Comforter has come, oh spread
the news around wherever men are found, the Comforter has
come!" Another favorite song included these lyrics: "Fill me
now with thy hallowed presence, come oh come and fill me
now; joy unspeakable and full of glory." The singing was enthusiastic. There was speaking in tongues—using *glossolalia,*
the unknown tongues—and in languages that were known.
Bartleman tells of a missionary from the Philippines who became critical of the meeting and desired to discredit it. But
when he heard persons in that meeting speaking in dialects
from the Philippines, from some of the tribes that he was at-
tempting to penetrate, he recognized that God was at work. For
these people had not been to the Philippines, nor had they
studied the dialects.

Other critics from China, Russia, and other parts of the
world heard unlearned men and women, under the power of
God, speak in their languages, just as had been experienced in
the day of Pentecost. It was a marvelous experience. In the cos-
mopolitan atmosphere of Los Angeles, people heard the gospel
and the witness of God's truth in their own languages. From
1906 to 1909, people came from all over the United States and
from Africa and Europe. Those who came and experienced the
Holy Spirit baptism returned to their homes with fresh vision
and power. They were equipped for service with the message of
repentance, salvation, worship, healing, holy living, deliverance, and the baptism of the Holy Spirit.

But there were some excesses at Azusa, and the disorder was
sometimes unbearable. There were times when clearly no one

was in charge. On occasion, flesh and carnality seemed to predominate. There were satanic attempts to discredit what God was doing. There was also the emergence of pentecostal pride. Because of what God was doing, there was a sense that pentecostals were somehow better than those from whom they had separated.

The Missed Opportunities of Azusa

God did something powerful at the Azusa revival. During an era when racism, sexism, and classism were accepted as normal, the Azusa revival welcomed all races, classes, and sexes as equals. Blacks, whites, Asians, Hispanics, and other groups were represented in the worship and welcomed under the same roof at 312 Azusa. It was reported that as many as fifteen to twenty ethnic groups and nationalities would gather at the communion table. An observer wrote, "The color line was washed away by the blood of Jesus."[4] No wonder Parham, a racist who came to Azusa in 1907, was unhappy with the integration he observed. He was unhappy because it did not fit into his idea of how the church should look. He attempted to stop the movement of God, but he could not stop what God was doing. For a brief period there was answer to the prayer that Jesus offered to God in John 17. Regrettably, the power to speak in new tongues, to heal the sick, and to cast out demons was not appropriated to rebuke the spirit of division and racism that surfaced. In 1907, division emerged when C. H. Mason and C. P. Jones could not agree on speaking in tongues as the initial sign of being filled with the Holy Spirit. They failed to appropriate the Holy Ghost's power to resolve the conflict, so the first major separation occurred as a result of a conflict between the two black leaders. Mason became the leader of the Church of God in Christ, and C. P. Jones separated and became the leader of the Church of God Holiness. The two men continued to be on friendly and speaking terms, but somehow they missed God. They should not have broken their relationship. There was no need for another denomination. God had put them together.

Another division arose, not about speaking in tongues, but about race. Segregation laws prohibited blacks, whites, and

Hispanics from social or spiritual mixing. The laws in Arkansas, Mississippi, Georgia, Alabama, and throughout the South said blacks and whites could not worship together. In 1914, Bishop Mason met with the white elders ordained in the Church of God in Christ. In that historic meeting in Hot Springs, Arkansas, white and black brothers in Christ failed to understand the burden of history and the opportunity to speak biblical truth to the powers of racism and segregation. It was a *kairos* moment, when the course of U.S. history could have been changed. A fatal choice was made to conform to the racist laws rather than to resist. God had spoken; he had manifested his power. He had revealed his will for a united church. For a moment, suppose the white, brown, and black brethren had appropriated the Holy Ghost's power they had received to oppose the evils of segregation and racism. From 1906 to 1914, the Church of God in Christ was racially mixed. Suppose the whole Pentecostal, Holiness movement, which today numbers more than four hundred million, had mustered the courage of Martin Luther or Dietrich Bonhoeffer, Martin Niemoller and Martin Luther King, and had declared to the powers in each state, "We are brothers and sisters. We are in covenant, we will not be separated by your laws. We are members of the family of God. We will worship and minister and fellowship together or we will go to jail together or we will die together. Here we stand, so help us God." Without doubt such a position would have resulted in lynchings and martyrdom, but God's truth would have won in the end. Then the civil rights movement would have been fought on spiritual grounds, and the church would have fulfilled Christ's mandate to be salt in a society lacking flavor and light in the darkness. God visited America in the Azusa revival in an unlikely place, a former stable. He used unlikely servants, including the sons and daughters of slaves. This movement had the potential of being God's solution to the American dilemmas of racism, sexism, and classism.

My thesis is that the leaders of this movement missed a date with divine destiny in Hot Springs. The same opportunity was given by God as had been given to the Protestant reformers and the leaders of the Great Awakening. Their decision not to trust God and to follow their conscience resulted in great social, spiritual, and economic changes in society. I believe there was the potential for the healing of the wounds from the Civil War and from the years of slavery, as well as the potential for God's power for forgiveness and reconciliation to be demonstrated. Imagine what could have been. The Klan would not have had the support of white Christians. There would have been no need for the emergence of the black Muslim groups. The energy of the civil rights movement could have been focused on evangelism, education, and economic development. There would have been no letter from the Birmingham Jail. No final sermon, "I've been to the mountaintop," delivered at the national headquarters of the Church of God in Christ Mason Temple. There seems to be a historical connection between a bad decision by spiritual leaders in Hot Springs in 1914 and the fifty-four years of segregation and suffering that culminated in the death of Martin Luther King in Memphis, Tennessee, in 1968.

Those who met in Hot Springs were undoubtedly good men, saved men, but they did nothing to correct the evils that prevented brothers and sisters from worshiping and serving their God together. Edmond Burke once said that "the only prerequisite for the triumph of evil is that good men do nothing." Jesus had left clear instructions: "I made you one. I brought you together, stay together." But a decision in Hot Springs was made to deny the mandate of Christ and to go separate ways based on skin color and ethnicity. May God help us to obey Scripture rather than listen to the directions of culture. May God help us to stay together.

While it is true that the Pentecostal, Holiness leaders who had experienced the miracle of Azusa missed the opportunity to lead our nation in the godly resolution of the American dilemma of racism, it may be that God will give another opportunity to experience this transforming and unifying power of the Holy Spirit. The acknowledged leader of this great revival was a black man, W. J. Seymour, the son of a slave. Other sons and daughters of slaves participated equally with sons and daughters of slave owners and confirmed segregationists. For a few years, from 1906–14, Pentecostal, Holiness believers from many ethnic backgrounds in the United States believed and saw many miracles of salvation, healing, deliverance from demon possession, and so on, as well as the "washing away of the color line in the blood of Jesus." What God had started was hindered by a carnal and unfortunate decision to conform to culture rather than to affirm unity in the family of God and to suffer if necessary.

It may be that the miracle of Memphis in 1994—when the leaders of several Pentecostal, Holiness denominations met, confessed, repented, washed each other's feet, and pledged to be reconciled—was a signal that we are to revisit Azusa and complete the unfinished business of racial reconciliation.

Now it is time to prayerfully consider the next step to realize the vision of unity and justice that was only beginning when it was aborted in 1914. The following recommendations are respectfully submitted to the pentecostal and charismatic churches of North America:

1. Call for the praying women and all intercessors for a fresh move of God in our day.
2. Affirm and reestablish throughout all of our churches the observance of the annual Feast of Pentecost as a major holy day. The leadership of denominations could call for three days of fasting and prayer leading up to Pentecost Sunday. Further, in every city where there are representative churches, there could be a joint service in a local civic auditorium. It would be an annual celebration in every community to worship, to preach, and to witness salvation and miracles that would enhance the local Pentecostal, Holiness witness and demonstrate unity.
3. Appoint a commission of theologians, scholars, and pastors to report on the impact of the miracle of Memphis on participating denominations and on what has happened in the decade since.
4. Enter into covenant to mutually recognize ordination of elders and pastors.
5. Call for papers on history, theology, and ethics to be presented at each annual convocation. These papers would be edited and published. Through this process mature writers and scholars would be encouraged and new talent would be discovered.

6. Include representation from participating denominations on all college, university, and seminary boards, with the intent of sharing resources.
7. Recruit students and provide college and seminary scholarships, when appropriate, to minorities.
8. Whenever possible engage in joint ventures in foreign and domestic missions and evangelism; for example, in the United States a national and local strategy could be developed to address homelessness, hunger, AIDS, and social, economic, and environmental injustice.
9. Remain open always to fresh ideas from heaven so that a healthy balance of word and spirit will save us from the extremes of cold formalism or hot fanaticism.

May God help us to redeem the time, because the days are evil (Eph. 5:16).

5

The Pentecostal Vision
for Christian Unity

Cheryl Bridges Johns

One of the heroes of faith depicted in the dome mural of the chapel of Beeson Divinity School is William J. Seymour, the founder of the Azusa Street Mission, which is also known as the fountainhead of our movement—the pentecostal movement. We should not forget that Azusa Street was a scandalous event. It was scandalous for several reasons. It was scandalous that women preached and prophesied. It was scandalous that denominational lines seemed to be irrelevant. It was scandalous that poor people and rich people worshiped together.

In particular, it was a scandal at the turn of the twentieth century for people of different races, "colored people" and "white people," to worship together. But at the Azusa Mission they did worship together, embracing one another with a fervent love that seemed to wash away the color lines. Reports in the *Los Angeles Times* would take note of how "Negro washerwomen" and white businessmen were embracing. For the reporters such things clearly indicated that the revival was an affront to decency and proper Christian decorum.

The vision of racial unity that was at Azusa Street was based upon the belief that humanity was living in the end times as spoken of by the prophet Joel and that God was pouring out his

Spirit upon all flesh (Joel 2:28). The Azusa participants believed that the Holy Spirit was at work renewing the message and meaning of the day of Pentecost. Pentecost for them was not a day that came and went, but rather a day that came and stayed. It is a continuing festival that was inaugurated on the day of Pentecost. It was not one day, it is *the* Day, and it is *the* Day of the Lord.

The world saw this event as Babel—confusion of tongues, mixing of races, confusion of gender roles. Early pentecostals saw this as the coming of the kingdom of God. In many ways they understood the events surrounding their movement as reversing the curse of Babel. At Pentecost, they saw created a new unified language—a language of the Spirit. A language that both the articulate, educated and the illiterate, uneducated could speak together. A language that dismantled, as the deconstructionists tell us today, the self's last hiding place, language, and levels all people and all humanity and tongues. It was a language that brought unity and transcended racial and ethnic boundaries.

The language of Pentecost represents not chaos, but order. It is an order that could not be recognized by the world that chose to name its own chaos as order. Harvey Cox, speaking of this power, says in his book *Fire from Heaven* that the pentecostal vision has the ability to "lure chaos into the sacred circle and contain it." In this sense, Pentecost confronts chaos that is found in the world and transforms it into order.

At the dawn of the twenty-first century, it is common now in many ecumenical and theological circles to speak of Pentecost as the cure for the postmodern world of Babel. This is true in many different circles, and it is now fashionable to speak of the vision of Pentecost as the great festival that renews all of creation bringing order out of chaos and uniting a great divided and broken humanity. These new discussions have caused me—a fourth-generation pentecostal—to reexamine my own tradition's vision of Pentecost and to put it in dialogue with some of the current visions.

It should be noted that pentecostals do not have rights to Pentecost. We, who have chosen to name ourselves after this great festival, must understand that Pentecost belongs to the one, holy, catholic church. As Pope John Paul II says, Pentecost gives the church her life and continues to renew the church daily. It is with this awareness that I offer some of the basic elements of the pentecostal vision of reality. I want to describe quite briefly our vision of unity, a vision in keeping with the formative experience and outpouring of the Holy Spirit in the Azusa revival. I would also like to utilize a typology developed by my colleague Steven Land, who refers to pentecostal spirituality within a dialectic of fission and fusion.

In terms of fusion, pentecostals understand that under the umbrella of Pentecost there is a uniting of what has been divided by sin. The divisions that are now in the world regarding race, class, and gender are bridged by Pentecost. While Pentecost does not deny ethnic or gender identities, it takes away the inherent warring for preeminence that is found in humankind. Indeed, the cleansing of Pentecost fire prevents the fires of ethnic cleansing. It is not insignificant that the father of the pentecostal movement was an African American son of a former slave. It is not insignificant that the location of the Azusa Street Revival was a rented hall in a part of Los Angeles where there were many immigrants and poor people. The revival brought about a fusion of all the things that the world seeks to keep divided. In doing so, it unleashed a redemptive power that does reverse the curse of Babel. This, despite the fact that the children of this revival have failed to live up to its originating vision.

Within the pentecostal tradition (especially in North America) we are guilty of succumbing to the pressures of our society. There were *kairos* moments, like the meeting at Hot Springs, Arkansas, when we failed to live up to our primal vision, and thus the founding ideal of racial reconciliation gave way to a harsh legacy of segregation and prejudice. In our desperation for acceptance we have made great compromises. In addition to racial reconciliation, I believe we have missed an opportunity to model gender reconciliation. Slowly, over the decades, the prominent role of women was diminished.

Another lost moment was when pentecostals became part of the National Association of Evangelicals. Here we compromised in the area of gender equality. In order to be part of a "brotherhood" we learned to relegate our sisters to the more acceptable "women's auxiliaries." Women who preach and teach have been an affront to the controlling evangelical paradigm, and the pentecostals learned quickly that the dominant role women played in our movement would not gain us favor either in polite society or within the evangelical "brotherhood." These moments can never be regained; however, there is the continuing grace of renewed vision.

In addition to the fusion regarding racial and gender divisions, Pentecost brings about a fusion of people from various Christian traditions. R. G. Spurling, the founder of the Church of God (Cleveland, Tennessee), was a Baptist who spoke of this powerful fusion of Christians as being possible through what he called "the law of love." He understood creeds to be ultimately divisive and insisted that while the Protestant Reformation restored what he called "the law of faith," the church needed a further restoration of the "law of love."

A pentecostal vision of unity seeks the community of the Spirit that makes possible the prayer of Jesus in John 17. For many pentecostals this unity is somewhat fluid, with worship serving as the primary ecumenical vocation and prayer as a critical ecumenical task. Abiding together within the law of love would, on the one hand, celebrate the diversity of gifts that are found within the body of Christ, and, on the other hand, acknowledge the unity of truth and love. Herein lies the dynamic fission as well as fusion that are present in the fire of Pentecost.

Inasmuch as Pentecost contains both promise and judgment, this festival divides what is unhealthily joined as well as unites what is unhealthily divided. Peter's sermon on the day of Pentecost as recorded in Acts 2 is the prototype of both promise and judgment. The unity of Pentecost is based upon the rising Lord, and it calls for repentance and baptism (Acts 2:38). It is a unity that calls for a turning away from what the apostle Peter termed "this corrupt generation." Thus, Pentecost is a judgment against this world's refusal of Christ. It contains the apocalyptic fervor that speaks of signs in the earth below, blood and fire and smoky mist. The sun, warned Peter, would be turned to darkness and the moon to blood before the

coming of the Lord's great and glorious day. Pentecost, as the
narrator of Acts observes, cuts to the heart of everyone and
then calls for a decision. But it contains the great promise that
everyone who calls upon the name of the Lord shall be saved.
So it can be said that both the diversity and the limits of pentecostal unity may be found in Acts 2.

The fire of Pentecost brings about a unity of cosmic proportions: all flesh and the whole created order. However, this cosmic unity is centered in Christ. In Christ is the creation of the
"new Israel" in which the boundaries are redrawn by the Spirit
to include those previously marginalized and found outside the
gates. Notes the prophet Joel: "Then afterward I will pour out
my spirit on all flesh; your sons and daughters shall prophesy,
your old men shall dream dreams, and your young men shall
see visions. Even on the male and female slaves, in those days,
I will pour out my spirit" (Joel 2:28–29 NRSV).

For pentecostals, the limits of pentecostal unity again are
contained in Scripture. While we believe in ongoing revelation
(namely that the Spirit continues to speak through the distribution of various gifts), we hold to the canon of Scripture as the
final authority for the church. The limits of diversity are being
redrawn by many in ways that transgress the unity that is in
Christ. Such folk fail to see the power of fission (judgment) that
is contained in Pentecost. Pentecost is not a warm soup in
which everyone exists. Babel is not reversed by a discourse that
allows unholy tongues. So given the current ecumenical landscape, we are all called to test the spirits, to discern the body of
Christ, and to seek the joining of love and truth.

Permit me to do a bit of hypothesizing regarding our ecumenical future. It appears to me that the great ecumenical divide of the not-so-distant future will not be found so much between our various traditions as within our communions
themselves. One great divide is that between the so-called First
World and the so-called Third World or Majority World. Christianity is being reformulated in the southern hemisphere. This
reformulation will challenge those of us in North America to
relate to the new Christian faith that is young, urban, non-
white, and poor. Are we prepared to relate to this new face? I
think not. For the ways in which Christ is being experienced

beyond the bounds of what used to be known as "Western civilization" call us to look again at our standard theological formulations. For instance, among the world's dispossessed, who are seen almost as "nonpersons" in a global economy, salvation is not formulated primarily in terms of justification by faith. Salvation is being proclaimed as what the late Richard Shall called "the reconstruction of life in the power of the Spirit."[1] Salvation is the power to deliver people from demonic clutches and to heal lives characterized by abuse, addictions, and despair.

I would like to end my remarks with a story that to me serves as a prototype for the vision of Azusa Street that Bishop McKinney and I have attempted to describe. One of the visitors to Azusa Street was Reverend G. B. Cashwell, a minister of the Pentecostal Holiness Church in North Carolina who, in 1907, traveled by train across the United States to reach Los Angeles. He went seeking the baptism of the Holy Ghost. Upon arrival, Cashwell was taken back by what he saw. Not only was an African American in charge of the revival, but the majority of worshipers were black. Despite having traveled such a long distance, Cashwell decided to attend but not to participate in the services. During his first service at the mission, a young black man walked over to him and placed his hands on his head, praying for him to be "baptized with the Holy Ghost." This event, said Cashwell, "caused [a] chill to go down my spine." Being deeply prejudiced against blacks, Cashwell was confronted with a profound dilemma: to stay put with the presence of God among the poor, blacks, and Hispanics, or to leave without receiving the gift he had traveled so far to receive. Soon Cashwell "lost his pride" and asked Seymour and several young black men to lay hands on him. He was filled with the Holy Ghost and began to speak in other tongues. Cashwell returned to North Carolina a changed man. He became known as the "Apostle of Pentecost to the South," bringing with him a testimony of racial unity decades before civil society dared to envision the possibility.

A "subversive memory" of a vision of Christian unity exists within Pentecostalism. It is found among those who long ago walked a sawdust trail toward a new order of creation. May those of us who are their grandchildren find the same courage.

6

Who Is the Holy Spirit for Us Today?

THE PERSON AND WORK
OF THE HOLY SPIRIT IN JOHN 20:19–23

Glenn E. Davis

It was a hot summer in late August 1979. I was a member of a parachurch organization called the Agape Force, which conducted a training program named Crystal Springs Institute. As part of that program, each of us was required to participate in a mission trip. This mission trip was highly unusual. You and your team are dropped off in a Texas town with instructions to minister to whomever God brings in your path, to trust God for shelter and finances, and to rely on the Lord for safe return. The Agape Force ministry called the trip the "Weekend Mission," but the students called it the "Trust God or Die" weekend.

My four-man team was assigned South Dallas, and I did not know at that time what a rough area it was. For the first time in my life, I did not know where my next meal was coming from, with whom I would be staying, what was going to happen, and how I was going to get home. After getting off the bus, the first thing we did was pray. We were desperate. As we prayed, we felt that the Holy Spirit wanted us to begin at the beginning. So, we decided to start by evangelizing the first people we met on the street. My partner and I began to talk with an African American man who was obviously down and out.

As we shared, he grew more and more obstinate. The more we shared, the less effective I felt we were in reaching him. In fact, it seemed as if my words were dropping out of my mouth and straight onto the ground. I felt that I was not communicating the gospel clearly, effectively, or powerfully. Finally, in desperation, I said, "If a car hit you this afternoon, where would you go, to heaven or hell?" He just looked at me and began to curse.

I walked away feeling empty and helpless. I had no authority and power in my witness. I began to pray anxiously that God would somehow help me to be an effective testifier of God's grace. I did not want the weekend to be a waste. I needed divine intervention. Later that morning as the team moved north, we began to walk down Commerce Street. We were very conspicuous as we carried our Bibles in one hand and held on to our sleeping bags with the other. We turned and began to walk through a plaza where a number of executive-types were sitting on park benches eating sack lunches. Out from the crowd, a short, plump African American lady stood up and yelled, "What are you boys doing?" We replied that we were from Lindale, Texas, and we were out witnessing. At the top of her lungs, she cried out, "Have you ever been filled with the Holy Ghost?" I thought, "Oh, my goodness, we've got a live one." My team leader, who was standing in front of me, said, "Yes, I have." The team member bringing up the end said, "So have I." I thought, "Good, maybe she will leave us alone." Then without warning, the last member of the team shouted, "No, I have not!" I thought, "Why did you have to go and say that?" Immediately, she asked us to come over, so that she could pray for him.

This is the scene: four men in their early twenties kneeling in front of a park bench as this lady stands over one young man praying loudly in tongues. She was praying *very* loudly in tongues. As she began to pray, I asked the Lord whether this whole thing about the fullness of the Spirit was for real. The denomination in which I was raised discounted the gifts of the Spirit. I told the Lord that I did not want to resist anything if it was genuine, even if it seemed a bit bizarre. At that moment, I began to speak in tongues. Very gently and without great emotion, the Holy Spirit began to touch my heart and bless me with the sweetness of Jesus. My emotions were so subdued that I wondered whether my ministry team understood what God had done in my life. I was experiencing for the first time a fresh filling of the Holy Spirit with a manifestation of a spiritual gift. Already, God was answering my prayer from that morning; he was responding to my cry for his personal power, presence, and authority. Thank God for that little African American lady who was willing to be bold for Christ.

Overcoming Objections

I know that for many evangelicals, such an account is troubling. Let us examine some of the common objections that some have offered to my story.

"Are you saying *the* manifestation of being filled with the Holy Spirit is *glossolalia?*" No, 1 Corinthians 13 says that love is the distinguishing quality of the Spirit-filled life. However, in the Book of Acts, when an individual encountered the Holy Spirit, some type of vocal gift was usually manifested. Therefore, I would not be surprised if you did speak in tongues (or prophesied) as the Spirit blessed you with his presence. Gordon Fee says that the gift of tongues (i.e., *glossolalia*) was the *normal* experience of being filled with the Spirit in the first-century church, but that does not make it *normative.*[1] In other words, you probably will, but you are not a subpar Christian if you do not. *Glossolalia* was the common experience of New Testament believers, but not a mandated one.

Accurately, Jack Hayford has stated that the primary purpose of the charism of *glossolalia* is intimacy with our sweet and precious Savior, the Lord Jesus Christ. "At its core, the purpose of tongues is a matter of worship and praise."[2] When Hayford experienced *glossolalia* for the first time, he stated, "I was happy—not because of tongues, but because of Jesus! I knew He had patiently brought me beyond all doubt and fear, around tradition, past sensation and unto Himself."[3] If the Lord Jesus wants to give you a gift and that gift will bring you into a love relationship with him, then why not receive it? Many of our objections to the gift of tongues are based on its abuse, on our fears or our pride, but these doubts can be erased when we understand that the charism of *glossolalia* is for the purpose of having a closer, deeper, more devoted relationship with Jesus.

"Are you saying that for me to be a complete Christian, I need a second blessing or baptism of the Holy Spirit?" No, you are complete in Christ when you surrender your heart to the Lordship of Jesus. "For in Christ the fullness of God lives in a human body, and you are complete through your union with Christ" (Col. 2:9–10, NLT). However, I ask you, "Why not? Why not have continuous ongoing experiences of the Holy Spirit?" Peter and John were immersed in the Holy Spirit in Acts 2, then they cried out for more in Acts 4 and received God's blessing afresh. The original Greek emphasizes this truth in Ephesians 5:18, "Do not be drunk with wine, but be constantly filled to the point of being controlled by the Holy Spirit." Jesus was described as a man full of the Holy Spirit, and so was Stephen; Paul said, "For the kingdom of God is not food and drink but righteousness and peace and joy in the Holy Spirit" (Rom. 14:17, RSV). The Holy Spirit was the animating, life-producing, empowering presence of God in the first-century church. As Gordon Fee has stated, "The people of God as a community of believers owe their existence to their common, lavish experience of the Spirit."[4] They were the fellowship of the Spirit (1 Cor. 12:13), they stood firm in the Spirit (Phil. 1:27), they were enabled to love by the power of the Spirit (Rom. 15:30), and their unity was formed by Spirit's presence (Eph. 4:3). The Holy Spirit energized the first-century church; their common life involved his power, fruits, and gifts. Therefore, we are called to ongoing experiences with the Holy Spirit. He makes Jesus real, he gives fresh insight in the Word of God, he is strength in our weakness, and he is our taste of heaven on earth. As Oswald Chambers writes,

> The Holy Spirit is not a substitute for Jesus, the Holy Spirit is all that Jesus was, and all that Jesus did, made real in personal experience now. The Holy Spirit alone makes Jesus real, the Holy Spirit alone expounds His Cross, the Holy Spirit alone convicts of sin; the Holy Spirit alone does *in* us what Jesus did *for* us.[5]

It is a necessity for us to experience Jesus afresh by the personal presence and power of the Holy Spirit because we are fighting spiritual battles against sin, death, the world, the flesh, and the devil (Eph. 2:1–6). We need renewal, reform, and revival because we live in the midst of the fallout of the Fall.

The Challenge

This is the challenge: we need that same common lavish experience of the Holy Spirit that propelled the early church. We need the Spirit's fruit exhibiting Christ-like behavior in our lives. We need the manifestation of the charismata of the Spirit in order to demonstrate the wonderful love and power of God.

Barry Seagren quotes Martin Lloyd-Jones candidly asking his congregation,

> So we say, oh well, I am already baptized in the Holy Spirit; it happened when I was born again, it happened at my conversion. I have got it all! Got it all? I simply ask in the name of God, why then are you as you are? Got it all? Why then are you so unlike the New Testament Christians? Got it all? Got it at your conversion? Then, where is it, I ask?[6]

I am glad that I was not in his congregation that day, but I need to ask myself, "Am I living my life based on past experiences of Jesus' love or am I enjoying his sweet presence moment by moment?" Do others see the fruit of the Spirit in my life or a mere shadow of the life of Christ? Are the gifts of the Spirit relics of an age gone by or part of my ongoing experience? Who is the Holy Spirit for us today? How can we experience God's empowering presence afresh? Let us start by looking at the experience of the disciples in John 20.

The Disciples

> That evening, on the first day of the week, the disciples were meeting behind locked doors because they were afraid of the Jewish leaders. Suddenly, Jesus was standing there among them! "Peace be with you," he said. As he spoke, he held out his hands for them to see, and he showed them his side. They were filled with joy when they saw their Lord! He spoke to them again and said, "Peace be with you. As the Father has sent me, so I send you." Then he breathed on them and said

to them, "Receive the Holy Spirit. If you forgive anyone's
sins, they are forgiven. If you refuse to forgive them, they are
unforgiven." (John 20:19–23, NLT)

The apostle John, whom I believe is the author of this gospel,
writes chapter 20 with one concern in mind: Jesus desired to
restore the key love relationships in his life that were broken
as a result of Good Friday. John does not describe the miracles
found in the other gospels, but he focuses on people and their
genuine need for grace in the midst of deep despair.

In verse 19, we find *desperate disciples* who are failing the
Lord. The verse begins with the phrase "in the evening," indi-
cating that what takes place is later on Resurrection Sunday.
Mary had given them the report of Jesus' appearance that
morning, yet they still had no faith to believe. The disciples
were failing in their walk throughout that day even after hearing Mary's report. Fear of people (i.e., the Jews) caused the disciples to fall short in their ability to trust Christ with their circumstances. The Book of Proverbs declares, "Fearing people is
a dangerous trap, but to trust the LORD means safety" (29:25,
NLT). The disciples fell into that trap.

The hearts of the disciples were bound up, symbolized by
the "locked doors" of the Upper Room. The "locked doors"
were emblematic of the fear, desolation, and distrust in their
hearts. The disciples were failing even though Jesus had taught
them that he would rise from the dead; their focus was on their
circumstances instead of on the words of Jesus (Mark 8:31;
9:31; 10:34; Luke 9:21; John 2:19). They were dejected, despondent, discouraged, and deflated.

Their fears were not irrational, but real. The authorities always go after the council as well as the ringleader. However,
after three years having been trained by Jesus himself, they
failed to grasp the significance of that day. How will Jesus react
to them? Will he express his disappointment and call for the
Father to give him a new round of disciples? "They just don't
get it, Father. They are just too thick. I taught and taught and
taught them, and still they don't get it." No, he speaks a word
of grace to them by granting them peace.

In verse 20, Jesus is *peaceful presence* by being the Prince of
Peace. He greets them and ministers to their fears and anxi-

eties by speaking "peace." His greeting of "peace" was customary for the age, but took on special significance for this occasion. Christ's peace is not of this world. Christ's peace reaches deep into our hearts, bringing grace and healing to our woundedness. Fear and anxiety comes from failing the Father, but peace comes from the heart of the Father as an act of grace. "Peace I leave with you; my peace I give you. I do not give to you as the world gives. Do not let your hearts be troubled and do not be afraid" (John 14:27, NIV). When Jesus says "peace" he means peace; not only does he mean peace, but also he *gives* peace. "The *shalom* of Jesus is not a mere greeting but an authoritative declaration from the Son of God, a crucified word that produces the peace it proclaims."[7]

Then, "He showed them both his hands and his side"; the marks of Christ are the wounds of the cross. The disciples knew this was the real Jesus since he was the crucified Christ. "The disciples . . . rejoiced"; joy comes in experiencing and encountering the crucified and risen Savior. All fears of arrest, all the despondency, and all the self-absorption are defeated by the presence of the crucified God. Since Jesus defeated sin, death, and the devil, the disciples know he can overcome their problems.

Verse 21 says, "As the Father sent me so I am sending you"; it is *Christ's commission.* We are called by Christ to go forth into the world in the same way that Christ ministered in the world. We are to preach, heal, deliver, and sacrifice in the same manner Christ taught, ministered, and laid down his life. "What? How can Jesus require this kind of ministry from us? It is an impossible task! You don't understand; I can't do that." That is exactly the point! Christ's commission from the Father are the words of Isaiah 61 found in Luke 4: to release captives, to preach the good news, to heal the blind physically and spiritually, to set free the oppressed, and to proclaim the year of Jubilee (Luke 4:18–19). The ministry of Jesus is not something we can do. God never anticipated that we could successfully live the Christian life. God knows that we are weak, needy, and poor as paupers. He is patiently waiting for us to realize it! The Christian life is a dependent life. Jesus lived a dependent life, a life reliant on the Father. "Jesus replied, 'I assure you, the Son can do nothing by himself. He does only what he sees the Father doing. Whatever the Father does, the Son also does' " (John

5:19, NLT). That is why Jesus takes the next step of breathing on them.

Verse 22 says, "And with that he breathed on them and said, 'Receive the Holy Spirit.'" The disciples were called upon to *breathe his breath*. This sacramental sign of breathing harkens back to Genesis 2:7 and Ezekiel 37:9–10. Jesus is re-creating humankind from the Fall and resurrecting a dead people into a mighty army. Jesus is now re-creating the disciples; he is not patching them up and sending them out to do their best. He is making them, as Paul said, "new creations" (2 Cor. 5:17). Jesus is sending the disciples out as new people: he is sending them out by the power of the Holy Spirit. He is taking a rag-tag bunch of failing disciples and turning them into mighty soldiers.

In Luke 4:18, Jesus said, "The Spirit of the Lord is on me, because he has anointed me. . . ." Jesus performed his ministry by being utterly dependent on the Holy Spirit; how can we do better? Do we really think that one can live the Christian life by one's own cleverness, abilities, and natural talents? Messiah means "anointed one." People knew that Jesus was the Messiah because of the Spirit's presence. Jesus did not perform any miracles, heal any sick people, or begin his teaching ministry until after the Spirit's descent upon him at the Jordan River. If this was true of Jesus who was sinless, how much more dependent on the Holy Spirit are we who have been stricken by the Fall? Jesus never meant for us to fulfill his commission without experiencing his power. The outside world will only know that we are Christ's own by the activity of the Spirit in our lives.

Our Need

We are just like the desperate disciples for we, too, are distraught by Satan's temptations, distracted by the world, and despondent due to sin. We too need the Prince of Peace to grace us with the "peace that passes all understanding" so that our hearts can be set at rest in his presence. We too have a Christ-commission to go forth into the entire world as "little Christs," advancing our Father's kingdom. Like the disciples, we need to breathe his breath so that we can be equipped afresh to be about our Father's business. Therefore, the question begs itself,

"How do we move God to bless us with a fresh touch of his Spirit?"

As we have already seen, the disciples did not receive the Spirit because they were mighty men of valor, but because they were weak, burdened, and bound. On Resurrection Sunday, the disciples were not standing on God's word, or displaying great resolve against the enemies of God, or being counted among the great heroes of the faith. No, they were failing, and Jesus breathed on them the Holy Spirit as an act of grace. The Holy Spirit was not poured out because of anything that the disciples had achieved, but the Spirit was given because of Jesus' finished work on the cross (Acts 2:31–33). Our receiving the Spirit is not predicated on our performance, but on Christ's performance on the cross (Gal. 3:1–5).

The Persistent Neighbor

Therefore, let us look at Luke 11:5–13 and discern what Jesus would want us to do. The context of the chapter is prayer, with Jesus telling a parable describing a persistent neighbor. In that parable, the main character is the next-door neighbor who has suddenly received an unexpected guest. The neighbor is very needy because he lives in an age where food is not readily available. He has to care for his guest, and he does not have the resources to provide. He goes to his sleeping neighbor and asks for his leftover bread. The neighbor is perturbed. If he gets out of bed, he will awaken his family, who are all asleep in the same bed with him. Any parent knows the difficulty of getting a group of children to go to sleep, but now the needy neighbor wants to disturb them. Yet the sleeping neighbor does hand over his leftover bread because of the friend's *boldness*. Jesus commends the friend's boldness as a true characteristic of genuine prayer. All God wants us to do is to ask and to ask boldly! "Which of you fathers, if your son asks for a fish, will give him a snake instead? Or if he asks for an egg, will give him a scorpion? If you then, though you are evil, know how to give good gifts to your children, how much more will your Father in heaven give the Holy Spirit to those who ask him!" (Luke 11:13, NIV). How do we receive the Holy Spirit? We ask, and we ask boldly!

However, we must have a flexible attitude. Whatever type of bread the Father decides to give must be acceptable to us. Many times, we will say, "We want the bread of the Holy Spirit!" but when God gives it we say, "This is not the kind of bread we wanted!" "No, Lord, I wanted rye, wheat, or pumpernickel!" When the Holy Spirit comes, whatever gifts he wants to display through us, we must be willing to receive. Remember the gifts of the Holy Spirit are just that—*gifts*. Gifts are for blessing, for encouragement, and for spiritual growth. The purpose of the charismata is to bring you and me, as the body of Christ, into a deeper love relationship with Jesus. So, let us ask![8]

As with the disciples, all God desires is that we recognize that we are at our wit's end and we cannot go on any farther without him. All he waits for us to do is ask! Then he will come and pour his presence upon us, bathe us in his love, and display his great and mighty mercy. The Holy Spirit will come and will reveal Jesus to us. This afternoon, if you desire more of the Holy Spirit, pray boldly, and you will be filled afresh with the sweetness of his presence.

Conclusion

Bishop McKinney has challenged us with the story of the great Azusa Street Revival and the beginning of the pentecostal movement. He describes its racial harmony, its gender equity, and its spontaneity in worship. He portrays with great eloquence the tragedy of missed opportunities. With honesty and conviction, Bishop McKinney tells us how pentecostal leaders accepted the racist, sexist, and classist values of their day. In addition, he shares about changed lives and the joy in Christ that was received because of the charismata. With these things in mind, *boldly* we need to ask our heavenly Father for another Pentecost. We need a fresh experience of the best aspects of the Azusa Street Revival. Do we not need racial harmony, gender equity, and heavenly blessing? Do we not need God's grace to reverse the tragedy of missed opportunities? Do we not need his power to enable us to undo all the wrongs? Do we not need joy in the Lord, that overflowing, overwhelming, genuine delight in Jesus? Let us ask with *boldness* for a fresh outpouring of the Holy Spirit upon us!

Speaking of pentecostals, Cheryl Bridges Johns states, "For them, Pentecost was not a day that came and went, but rather a day that came and stayed." Yes, let us pray that a fresh experience of pentecostal grace will come and stay! Who is the Holy Spirit for us today? He is the same Christ-breathed Spirit of John 20, the same Spirit poured out at Pentecost, and the same Spirit released at Azusa Street. He is the same Spirit that brings unity among the races, develops equality among the sexes, and transports earthbound beings into heavenly places through worship and praise. We need a fresh touch of that same Holy Spirit, today! Therefore, let us pray, "Come Holy Spirit!"

Part 4

Evangelicals
and Roman Catholicism

7

Why Evangelicals and Catholics Belong Together

Richard John Neuhaus

Let me begin with some observations that, listening today, and not least of all to the exchange this morning on fundamentalism and the panel this afternoon on evangelicals in the mainline denominations, one is struck by how much it comes back to the question of ecclesiology, to that part of theology that is ecclesiology—the doctrine of the church.

While my friend Richard Mouw was speaking and while I was listening carefully, I was also leafing through the Baptist hymnal. I was seeing things I have missed in my life experience. In the back of it, I noticed there is a page that says: "How to become a Christian." And I think it has six steps there: to acknowledge that you're a sinner, to accept Jesus, and so on. Then it has a little paragraph at the bottom. It says: "[A]nd when you have become a Christian, then you should be baptized and find a church." Well, that's the heart of the matter. Is that really the right sequence?

Cardinal Ratzinger, the prefect for the Congregation of the Doctrine of the Faith, once impressed me very much when he said, "You know the difference between the Protestant and the Catholic faith is that for a Catholic, the act of faith in Jesus Christ and the act of faith in the church is one act of faith. For the Protestant, it is two acts of faith." And frequently it never gets around to the second: namely, the church, ecclesiology.

The Catholic sensibility is very different from our fundamentalist friend who so articulately and very intelligently set forth this notion of true churches and false churches—churches in the plural—some are true, some are false. In the Catholic understanding of church, in any serious theological sense, church has no plural. There are, to be sure, local churches that comprise the one church. But that church has no plural, just as Christ has no plural. There is one Christ, who is the head, and therefore by definition there can only be one church, one body of Christ.

The Catholic church has a very—some people would say relaxed; others might say casual; others, being less friendly, might say promiscuous—notion of how this reality of the church, the body of Christ, in fact is lived out in life. James Joyce was not a great Catholic theologian, but he had something right when he said, "The Catholic church is 'here comes everybody.' " It takes very little to get in. Indeed, nothing but the fact that one is a sinner in need of the Savior is required.

A Methodist friend in Chicago says that he is very tired of all of the criticisms and lambasting of Christians and of churches and so forth, and he says, "Of course we're rotten to the core." He said, "I would say that my ministry is to get all those hypocrites off the streets and get them into church where they belong!" That's a fine Catholic sensibility.

The problem we are addressing here is the scandal of Christian division. There are people who say that it really isn't a scandal at all. There are those who have taken a lead from market economics and who say that actually it is an enormous benefit to Christianity in America (and indeed one of the reasons for its being so much more vibrant than Christianity in Western Europe particularly) that it is divided into competing denominations, sects, and factions. Each of them has to go full tilt to get its market share and beat out the opposition. All of this can be explained in terms of cost-benefit analysis. I am all for market economics, but I think this a very perverse way of understanding Christ and his church. For what we are to bear witness to in the world is the possibility of a new kind of community.

In Catholic theology the way we put it is to speak of the church not simply as having sacraments, but as itself being a sacrament to the world, and in other traditions there are cognate ways of putting this. The church is to represent to the world a possibility that God has opened for humankind. The quality of our life together is part of the gospel that we proclaim.

Who we are—who we are together—is part of the gospel that we proclaim. There is no getting around the fact that our Lord surely intended, as he prayed, "they may all be one so that the world may see and believe that I am sent by you." This is to be a visible unity. This is to be seen, just as the maxim that "the world will know you by your love" refers to a visible love. It's not an invisible love. It is a touchable, palpable, documentable, recordable, everyday, quotidian reality—Christ and his church. Christ as his church through time. The living presence of Christ in his body. That is the scandal. The scandal is not that we are not brothers and sisters. The scandal is not that we are not one. The scandal is that we are brothers and sisters and we are one and we live as though we are not. That's the scandal.

There are many reasons why there is a certain skepticism about the very idea of ecumenism among evangelical Protestants and among self-consciously traditional Catholics. Conservative Protestants and traditional Catholics have tended to view ecumenism, for understandable reasons during most of the twentieth century, as being an essentially liberal project in which the primary mandate is not truth but niceness, in which the goal is not the glorification of God in Christ, but the negotiation and accommodation of differences. The result is a kind of a tapioca-pudding type of Christianity—a pudding that has no theme, and no truth, and nothing worth proclaiming, nothing worth living for or dying for. We all understand that caricature of ecumenism, and God knows—through the institutions of what was called the ecumenical movement from Edinburgh in 1910 through the World Council of Churches and its many similar organizations—there is much to support that caricature. We can stipulate that, as the lawyers say, and then move beyond. But we cannot let whatever caricatures of ecumenism justly exist, or whatever abuses and distortions have been perpetrated in the name of ecumenism, compromise our devotion and obedience to the clear word of Jesus Christ and the word of Holy Scripture. That Jesus intends his church to exemplify the love and the unity and the transcendent hope, which is part of the gospel proclamation to the whole world, this is fundamental.

Evangelicals and Catholics Together is a project begun back in the early 1990s by Chuck Colson and me. In trying to coordinate this marvelous community of evangelical Protestants and Catholics, we did not think of ourselves as instituting a new movement. We believed then, and we believe now, that the initiation of this is the work of the Holy Spirit. There was a preparing of the ground through what Timothy George has called "the ecumenism of the trenches."

It is a remarkable thing and a great thing for all of us to consider. For those Catholics who despair of the possibility of significant Catholic influence in the transformation of our culture, and for those evangelicals who have their own doubts about Christianity's public witness, it is a great thing to remember that we have already seen, we see today in this country and in the world, the evidence of what can happen when Christian forces converge in truth. This convergence is in devotion to truth and the acknowledgment that there can never be a contest between unity and truth.

The truth of God in Jesus Christ is the promised unity of humankind, and the unity that we already possess is our unity in Christ. This we have seen already in action, *Deo gratias*, in the building of the pro-life movement. There would be no pro-life movement in America today—there would be no pro-life movement in the world today—were it not for the witness of evangelicals and Catholics here in the United States.

This is happening, and it is the initiative of the Holy Spirit. Chuck Colson and I believed that right from the beginning. The beginning of ECT was concern for what was happening in Latin America. Both Chuck and I spent considerable time there. It was, and is still, a pretty grim situation in terms of the relationship between evangelicals and Catholics. It is a situation of people not simply not bearing witness to the love of God in Christ together, but bearing witness against it, daily, bloodily.

Frequently, let it be said, this conflict came at the initiative of Catholic leadership, where evangelicals were viewed as encroaching upon Catholic territory in parts of Latin America. People were being driven out of their villages if they became evangelical Protestants. But, of course, on the other side there is always more than enough blame to go around. For example, there were and are vicious attacks upon the Catholic Church as the antichrist, as the very whore of Babylon, and all of that. To be freed from Catholicism is, in this view, essential to salvation.

So it was this circumstance in Latin America that initially spurred our collaboration. But we also realized that we still had a lot of work to do here in the United States, so ECT became primarily a project here in North America, but with spin-off groups working in Ireland, in Western Europe, and in large numbers of places in Latin America.

In 1994, we published the statement "Evangelicals and Catholics Together: Toward a Common Mission in the Third Millennium." We talked a lot about the culture wars, about the conflict between the culture of life and the culture of death and other issues that all Christians had to address in public. But the most important affirmation in that document is the simple statement that we recognize one another as brothers and sisters in Christ. And that, of course, came in for a good deal of criticism. Many evangelicals had not been reared to think of Roman Catholics, of papists, as brothers and sisters in Christ. However, especially with this pontificate, major changes were underway. One of the leading Southern Baptist officials, in about the third year of the pontificate of John Paul II, got me aside sort of grudgingly, and said, "You know, those guys really got a pope who knows how to pope!" It is worth noting that some of the most vigorous, dare I say at times virulent, critics of ECT have come from a particular slice of the Reformed Calvinist tradition, as distinct from the Wesleyan and various Holiness and pentecostal traditions.

People sometimes ask, "Has there been much opposition to ECT among Roman Catholics?" And the answer is, "No, not really." Why? Because to come back to my opening remarks, Catholics are somewhat promiscuous in their understanding of church. We're in conversation with everybody. Sometimes this is resented. We are asked, "How can you talk with so-and-so and with so-and-so?" Well, because by definition, if the Catholic Church is what she claims to be, which is to say catholic, she must be encompassing of the whole. And so we pursue dialogue with all other Christians, but also with Jews and with other world religions as well.

It is the firm Catholic belief that, in fact, the grace of God is by no means limited to the boundaries of the Roman Catholic Church. Wherever someone is savingly related to Jesus Christ, they must, by definition, in some ecclesiologically significant way, be related to the church of Jesus Christ. As Saint Paul says, nobody says Jesus Christ is Lord except by the Holy Spirit. Wherever there is that confession, the Catholic Church reaches out to someone who is, in an ecclesiologically meaningful sense, a brother or sister.

For there is only one church—visible, palpable, touchable, smellable, frequently laughable. Yes, the church sometimes seems ridiculous, if you look at the whole phenomenon of two thousand years through history, if you consider the maddening variety, contradictions, and conflicts that go under the banner of Christianity, encompassing two billion people in the world today.

When we look at all of that, we are tempted to say, only half tongue in cheek, "Our Lord has a lot more to answer for than we do." I mean, he started all this. Did he not intend to establish a church? Did he not intend to designate twelve pillars, apostolic pillars of that church? Did he not intend a continuing community that would be defined by its proclamation, by its prayer, by its life, and by its communion with the apostles? And did he not intend that of the apostles, Peter be given the commission to strengthen the brethren? And did he not intend that this would continue through time? That there would be successors to these apostles? And successors to Peter? And that this community, so apostolically structured, would go on in its wayward, sometimes triumphant, sometimes stumbling, but undoubtedly commissioned way of its Lord and Savior Jesus Christ?

What does the Catholic Church claim? The Catholic Church claims that it is the church of Jesus Christ most fully and rightly ordered through time. This is why it supports the goal of full communion among all Christians. Full communion means that we would be together at the altar, at what the Second Vatican Council calls the source and summit of the church's life. It would require our agreement in the unity of faith, our agreement in the unity of the liturgy enacted, in all its admitted diversity through the centuries, and it would require being in communion with Peter, the bishop of Rome, the two hundred and sixty-fourth steward of the Petrine ministry. John Paul II acknowledges in the encyclical *Ut Unum Sint* that the Petrine ministry has often been viewed as an obstacle to Christian unity, and not without reason. Thus, in a remarkable statement, the holy father has said to all separated Christians, "I invite you to join with me in rethinking how this Petrine ministry can find a better form, a more adequate form that will serve our unity, that will advance the fulfillment of communion that already exists between us."

Thus ECT has to deal with issues of theology and ecclesiology as well as our common concerns in society in terms of social witness and so forth. Yes, of course, we are talking about shared tasks, about the ecumenism of the trenches, and about the everyday contestation for decency in our public life, for sound moral education and for many other things that we Christians ought to be contending for together. But all of this presupposes theology.

After our first ECT statement in 1994, the critics said, "What's this business about your being brothers and sisters in Christ? You haven't established that. What about justification by faith, the Council of Trent, and so on?" We took those questions seriously, and, after several years of study and discussion, we have produced a document called "The Gift of Salvation." This document attends very adequately, I think, to what I as a Lutheran pastor and a Lutheran theologian understood to be the intent of the Lutheran Reformation, namely, that under the banner of justification by grace alone through faith alone by Christ alone, there arose not a call for separation but a reforming movement within and for the one church of Christ. Since then, our ECT discussion has moved forward to consider the long-debated controversy over Scripture and tradition. Out of this exchange has emerged a new statement published now in a book called *Your Word Is Truth* (Eerdmans, 2002).

In all of this, are we moving toward full communion or are

we simply removing the more obvious scandals of our divisions and creating certain patterns for collaboration? I don't know. If it is the work of the Holy Spirit, and if it is the intent that there be one community that is part of the gospel proclamation to the world of the promised unity of humankind, then surely it has something to do, even in its bits and pieces, with the movement toward full ecclesial reconciliation. Those involved in the ECT process have no illusion that our work is going to achieve some great dramatic breakthrough. Nor do we have any plans for reorganizing any of the major religious institutions. We simply recognize under the guidance of the Spirit the gift of unity that is ours as brothers and sisters in Christ. We believe that we ought to start living that way and so we will continue.

Every step of the way we know that this is not our work. It is our work only insofar as it is the work of Christ before it is our work. Every step of the way, we remind ourselves that there cannot be any conflict between unity and truth. The only thing that truly brings us together in Christ is the truth. As Cardinal Ratzinger has reminded us, our spiritual fathers who were at one another's throats over their disagreements about the truth during the great conflict of the sixteenth century were in fact closer to one another in Christ than those in our day who, in the name of Christian unity, ignore the truth. To disagree intelligently, respectfully, energetically, candidly about the truth is to achieve a greater level of unity than the unity that is bought at the price of pretending that the truth does not matter.

What is God doing through ECT? What would full communion even look like? I don't know. Nobody knows. But always, always haunted and driven by the prayer of our Lord in John 17, looking ahead to his sufferings and death, reflecting on what it would all mean, what it would all come to, he said, "I pray for them. I pray for them that they may be one as you and I, Father, are one, so that the world may believe." What we are doing in ECT will be, God willing, an instrument in some small way of the realization of that prayer, for Christian unity is part of the Great Commission. Our task is not to speculate about what our efforts may mean over the next ten years, fifty years, or who knows, if it pleases God to tarry, over the next hundred years or over the next millennium. Our task is that of obedience.

When I think about the work of ECT and the quest for Christian unity, as of so much else, I always remember the words of T. S. Eliot in his *Four Quartets*, "For us, there is only the trying. The rest is not our business." There are some who may take Eliot's phrase as a sigh of resignation, a shrug of the shoulder. After all, what can we do? But that is to miss its meaning, I think. For that line, "For us there is only the trying, the rest is not our business," is an exalted statement of faith. The rest is God's business, and we are not God. Thank God we are not God. Thank God, God is God!

8

The Gospel Call to Common Witness

Jeffrey Gros

As a Roman Catholic growing up in Southern Baptist Memphis, Tennessee, I always knew I was a Christian, born again by water and the Holy Spirit. We were always taught that we were saved by the unique sacrifice of Jesus Christ on the cross, which we participated in by the gift of his grace responded to in faith. When I was asked to date my conversion, I would always write my baptismal date in my friends' Bible, the day on which I was baptized by the church as an infant. Of course, I had recognition of this grace at moments of salvation's assurance, like at first communion and confirmation, and marvelous intimate recognition of God's loving experiences in teenage retreats, and more mature convictions into adult life.

However, most fellow Christians were "different" for us Catholics. As a child I learned the Calvinist understanding of salvation from Baptist neighbors who had memorized it in Sunday School. The understanding was called TULIP, a mnemonic device standing for total depravity, unconditional election, limited atonement, irresistible grace, and perseverance of the saints. We always felt that this doctrine was somewhat strange, since we were taught that grace was about God's loving care for us, which we experience every day in the celebration of the Lord's Supper, in which Jesus came to us to share his death and resurrection with us in our lives each day. I must say, in those early days, when we would pray Psalm 23, in its King James Version, and the Lord's Prayer together, I never thought that Baptists were less Christian or that there were some Baptists who doubted my Christianity.

I did find it strange when some of our African American "help" around the house claimed that their church went back to John the Baptist, before our church, which was founded on the apostles. It was only in university that I learned of the "Landmark" doctrine of some Baptists that traced congregations back to Jesus' times, like the Catholic doctrine of "apostolic succession" that claims bishops developed in the church as successors to the apostles, to oversee the teaching of the church and fidelity to the Bible from the earliest days of Christianity.

We knew that some preachers, like Dr. R. G. Lee, and Dr. Ramsey Pollard at Bellevue Baptist Church, did not like Catholics for some reason, especially during the 1960 election. Of course, there have now been three Southern Baptist presidents and only one Catholic, even though the demography of our country would suggest a different balance. I only learned later that Baptists have not always thrown their weight around politically, and that the Baptist tradition gave us in the United States the great legacy of religious liberty, and the separation of church and state enshrined in our First Amendment.

Since 1973, with the coming of Dr. Adrian Rogers to the pulpit of Bellevue Baptist in Memphis, we have not seen the preaching against Catholics with which I grew up. In fact, many of our Catholic neighbors go to a nine o'clock mass in order to hear him preach on television at eleven. Although his first sermon was "There Is No Social Gospel," his congregation has had a great social impact, and gave strong support to the Moral Majority, in the 1980s, with the leadership of Baptist layman Dr. Ed McAteer. Somehow, I always suspected that Baptists had certain values they took to the ballot box, and these values gave us a social climate, as a minority, with which we all had to live.

The rise of the so-called religious right and the evangelical vote was only recognizing what was, in fact, the case in my life for years. Finally acknowledging that evangelicals had their own version of a "social gospel" was not a negative or new learning for me, nor was it a surprise as it may have been for some secular political types. Catholics share many of the gospel values that are important to evangelicals. There are other issues on which our interpretation of the gospel differs markedly. On these latter we are called to conversation in Christ. When I returned to Memphis to teach after graduate studies, in 1971, I was amazed and gratified to see a pastors' dialogue between Catholics and Southern Baptists. Catholics had a great revival, culminating in 1965, with the end of the Second Vatican Council. Among other values in this revival was a priority for Bible study, lay leadership, advocacy of religious liberty, and outreach to fellow Christians in love and truth. The obvious fellow Christians in Memphis were the Baptists. While this dialogue did not endure, given changes in Baptist leadership, the personal and spiritual relationships did. I think the Catholic priests who attended these meetings were enriched by the deep faith and firm conviction of the Baptist pastors. In many congregations and parishes the relationships continue and deepen.

When the Supreme Court handed down *Roe v. Wade* in 1973, the Catholic diocese (which included the western third of Tennessee) organized a great gathering of ten thousand Catholics in the Memphis Coliseum to pray and mobilize for the protection of unborn human life. I had suggested to Bishop Carroll T. Dozier that we approach some of our evangelical Christian colleagues, including Dr. R. Paul Caudill, of First Baptist Church, on Parkway (there are fourteen "First" Baptist churches in the phone book!), to join with him in signing the pastoral letter "Choose Life." However, with all of the tensions in the Catholic Church over other ethical issues, like support of racial equality—unpopular in this "capital of the Delta"—and world peace, it was decided that this should be a moment of Catholic solidarity. We did read, however, during the communion service a passage on the sanctity of life by Dietrich Bonhoeffer, the German Lutheran martyr of the Nazi era.

Indeed, for many years the Baptist ethos permeated the part of the South in which I was raised. In studying the 1925 Southern Baptist Convention, which met in Memphis, and which adopted the "Baptist Faith and Message," I came to understand what was at stake, not only for the Baptist community but for the whole of Southern culture in these debates. While E. Y. Mullins was able to shepherd a more "moderate" confession through the convention than the likes of fundamentalist J. Frank Norris would advocate, a solid core of classical Christianity was affirmed against what was seen as the erosion of Christian values by northeastern secularist forces, especially in public education.

When one studies the South after the Civil War, with its poverty and rural environment, it is the churches in both the black and white communities that were the bulwarks of education. Many of the public-school teachers were preachers or Sunday School teachers on the weekends. The Southern Baptist Sunday School Board (now LifeWay Christian Resources) can be counted as one of the principal sources of literacy across the South. All of us who have grown up in places like Memphis must recognize the debt owed to the Southern Baptists for the cultural integrity and religious sensibilities that were maintained during this period.

Today, the Southern Baptist Convention, and other southern churches like the pentecostals, are worldwide communions living in a variety of cultures around the globe. Likewise, the "solid" South is no longer the "Bible Belt" as uniformly as it once was before modern transportation, migration, and communications brought enormous changes to the regions. This new pluralism has been unsettling for some evangelicals, like the new evangelical strength in numbers and political clout across the nation has been unsettling for those who do not have the positive experience of fellow Christians whose faith and experience is evangelical.

Evangelicals can be enriched by exposure to Christians in other traditions, as other Christians can learn from convinced, articulate, and open evangelicals. Christians can be enriched by sharing their faith, either through evangelism or in a dialogue of mutual respect, with fellow Americans who are not Christian. Pluralism can be understood as God's way of helping us deepen our Christian conviction and teaching us to be more articulate about our faith and to be better evangelists.

Catholics in particular need to learn from Baptists and from

other evangelical Christians how best to evangelize the nonbe-
liever. Certainly Billy Graham has been an ecumenical model
for us all. Since the 1964 Boston Crusade, when Cardinal Cush-
ing appeared on the platform with Dr. Graham to endorse the
crusade, Catholics have appreciated the opportunity to collab-
orate in common witness for the gospel. Dr. Graham and his
organization have always been very serious about returning the
names of the converted to their church leaders, including
Catholics.

One more personal story before discussing the importance
of formal developments that have occurred between Catholics
and evangelicals. When I returned to Memphis in 1971, I was
teaching at Memphis Theological Seminary, a Cumberland
Presbyterian school, with a Methodist majority in the student
body and an ethos that was Southern evangelical. Two incidents illustrate the challenges of Catholic and evangelical relations in this context.

First, I was teaching "History of Christian Thought," using
a standard Protestant seminary textbook. After looking at the
textbook, and hearing that I was a Catholic, one of the students
felt the need, in conscience, to drop the class. His explanation
was that he was pentecostal and fundamentalist, and therefore
could not take my class. From that time on I would introduce
myself, at the beginning of a class, as a Bible-believing Christian in the Roman Catholic tradition.

Second, after a successful city revival in which a number of
our students were actively involved, one of my students suggested that the school ought to have a statement of faith to
which all teachers and students should subscribe. Rather than
being concerned about "thought control," or encouraging this
initiative for orthodoxy, I asked the student to consider a variety of options. Should the school require everyone's subscrip-
tion to the Cumberland Presbyterian confession of faith, even
though a minority of students belonged to the sponsoring
church? Should the school use an ecumenically constructed
confession, possibly from those used in the World Council of
Churches? Or should the classical Niceno-Constantinopolitan
Creed, which we were studying, be the flagship of orthodoxy
for the school?

Needless to say, the student had envisioned a few of the faculty and friends sitting down and concocting a "new orthodoxy" for the needs of the day, rather than drawing on the "faith of the church through the ages" as the norm for our common confession. This situation taught me that the energy of evangelical commitment could only be enhanced by a deepening of the theological content of that faith and an appreciation of Christian history, which is so dear to us all.

I was amazed when I was asked to teach the course on church and sacraments. This was in the 1970s before the classical ecumenical text *Baptism, Eucharist, and Ministry*[1] and the World Council of Churches' document *The Nature and Purpose of the Church*.[2] In class we had to use a general history; Avery Dulles's *The Models of the Church*, which outlined emphases that would correspond to the different traditions represented in the class; and the constitutions, books of disciplines or worship, and confessions of faith of the class members. In that context as a professor, I had to help Methodists understand why they did not rebaptize Christians coming from other churches, and Disciples of Christ students why their church often did.

In this course it was also a revelation to me that students wanted to cover those other ministries that Catholics call sacraments, even when they had been redefined at the Reformation. All of the Protestant students were ordained or moving toward ordination in their churches. They performed marriages, ministered to the sick, reconciled sinners, and held confirmation classes. Therefore, they were interested in what resources there were in the Scripture and the faith of the church through the ages for informing their ministry and understanding the biblical and liturgical bases for these Christian rituals. Indeed, I am sure we all learned from one another in clarifying how the gospel was embodied in our diverse approaches to these evangelical ministries.

Today it is much easier to teach such courses in a mixed context of students. The texts produced by biblical and historical scholars working together outline both commonalities and differences and lay a groundwork for our gospel ministry. These works also outline issues that are still in need of resolution as we move deeper into that communion for which Christ prayed.

Evangelical and Catholic Common Witness

While there may be a great gulf in the experience of many between evangelical and Catholic expressions of the Christian faith, it is clear that we share much more than separates us. Furthermore, it is quite clear that the urgency of the spread of the gospel of Jesus Christ demands more common witness of us than we have the resources for from our experiences.[3] In this section I review some of the more formal relationships.

Just as I was gratified, in 1971, to find a Southern Baptist–Catholic pastors' conversation in Memphis, Tennessee, so I have been blessed to know that there have been formal relations between Southern Baptists and Catholics in the United States, through the Home (now North American) Mission Board and the Committee for Ecumenical and Interreligious Affairs, since that same year; formal conversations since 1977;[4] and a variety of other developments in Catholic and evangelical relations.

Themes such as Scripture, ministry, spirituality, salvation, church, evangelization, social action, grace, baptism, eschatology, the Lord's Supper, discipleship, the communion of saints, authority, worship, and marriage were taken up in the early conversations between Southern Baptists and Catholics. With the new conservative leadership and an authorization of the conversation by the Southern Baptist Convention, discussions on Scripture were able to develop a report, recognizing that

> Southern Baptists and Roman Catholics believe in the Triune God, the Father, the Son and the Holy Spirit, and we confess the full deity and perfect humanity of Jesus Christ. We find these truths of faith in God's written Word, the Sacred Scriptures. While our two traditions differ with regard to the extent of the biblical canon, we cherish the Sacred Scriptures, use them regularly in our worship and devotion, and seek by God's grace to understand them more clearly.[5]

In this context common formulations on revelation, the Word

of God, inerrancy, inspiration, infallibility, the canon, historicity, methods of research, literalism, and fundamentalism were developed by the scholars from the two communities. These statements together did not attempt to minimize differences, but rather articulated what was held in common, where there were differences of definition, and where there were different understandings of the faith.[6]

These conversations in the United States have enabled international dialogues sponsored by the Baptist World Alliance and the Catholic Church.[7] The U.S. Southern Baptist–Catholic conversation ended in 2001, though many important relationships continue on local and institutional levels. Through the Glenmary Home Missioners, the Catholic Church in the United States has cultivated direct relations with Southern Baptists for more than thirty years, relations that will only deepen under the providence of God.

Southern Baptists, because of the size of the denomination, are able to work in isolation from other Christians. This is also true for Roman Catholics in many parts of the world. However, leaders in the Convention are aware of Baptist responsibility for collaboration with other evangelicals on behalf of the gospel.[8]

John Stott and other prominent evangelical leaders have produced a very important *Evangelical–Roman Catholic Dialogue on Mission*.[9] This dialogue has also enabled the World Evangelical Fellowship to enter into a conversation with the Catholic Church.[10] Of course, Roman Catholicism remains a flash point for many evangelicals, at a time when relationships are deepening and the world stands in need of common gospel witness.[11]

From the standpoint of this Bible-believing Catholic observer, the internal discussion of Christian faith generated by the 1994 "Evangelicals and Catholics Together"[12] can only engender more honesty and deepen concern for the truth of the gospel.[13] While this particular initiative does not break new theological ground and does not claim official sponsorship, it has created an interest in the evangelical world that will require years of dialogue and an intense scrutiny of previous prejudices that can only enhance mutual understanding and a richer gospel witness, if pursued with integrity and honesty by all involved.[14]

The 1999 signing, between officials of the Catholic Church and Lutheran churches around the world, of a *Joint Declaration on the Doctrine of Justification* has dramatic implications for all who take seriously God's saving love in Jesus Christ. At the very center of Luther's concerns in the sixteenth century was the question of justification by grace through faith and the problem of good works. Luther did not initially object to bishops or even the pope, and he clearly did not intend to divide the church. Unfortunately, discussions between Catholic and evangelical parties within the church had broken down by 1541, and new, separate communities emerged that have come to be called Protestant.

Since 1966 these discussions about what divides Christians have been taken up again, with a new seriousness about the biblical and theological pursuit of the truth of the gospel. Catholics have begun to find agreement with a variety of Reformation churches on issues that have divided Christians since the sixteenth century. The biblical and historical scholarship carried out by Lutherans and Roman Catholics has been most productive in resolving some of the Reformation debates. This historic development, emerging from studying again Paul's teaching on justification, the condemnations of Protestants and Catholics in the sixteenth century, and the present faith of the two churches, has enabled a level of agreement unexpected three decades ago.

On the basis of this research and dialogue, on a host of issues other than justification,[15] the churches have been able to move from common biblical study to official action. This action clarifies the truth that is shared, notes differences that continue—though not dividing the churches in the essentials of the faith—and enables Catholics and Lutherans whose churches have signed the declaration to recognize that the condemnations of the sixteenth century, on this subject, do not apply to one another:

> The Lutheran churches and the Roman Catholic Church have together listened to the good news proclaimed in Holy Scripture. This common listening, together with the theological conversations of recent years, has led to a shared under-

standing of justification. This encompasses a consensus in
the basic truths; the differing explications in particular statements are compatible with it.

In faith we together hold the conviction that justification
is the work of the triune God. The Father sent his Son into
the world to save sinners. The foundation and presupposition
of justification is the incarnation, death, and resurrection of
Christ. Justification thus means that Christ himself is our
righteousness, in which we share through the Holy Spirit in
accord with the will of the Father. Together we confess: By
grace alone, in faith in Christ's saving work and not because
of any merit on our part, we are accepted by God and receive
the Holy Spirit, who renews our hearts while equipping and
calling us to good works.[16]

These paragraphs are the core of a short document that witnesses to the common faith that is shared, and the hopes for
deeper communion building on this decision.

Of course, not all Protestant Christians will find because of
this agreement that they have resolved all of their concerns
with Catholics. However, it will be necessary for all honest
Protestants to assess the agreement and to pursue in dialogue
with Catholics what more they see as necessary to be faithful
to the gospel of justification as it is understood in the Scriptures. This agreement creates a new platform for dialogue and
a new opportunity to witness together to the grace of God in
Jesus that comes to us through faith. Many Catholics have
prejudices, coming from centuries of teaching, about Protestants and what they believe. Some Protestants still distort
what they think Catholics believe about good works. This declaration is a challenge for all to face one another in honesty and
openness.

A dramatic story that also illumines Catholic and evangelical relationships is that of the pentecostal encounter. Dr. David
du Plessis of the Assemblies of God attended the Vatican Council, not as a representative of pentecostal churches, but as an
individual.

In 1965, when the Second Vatican Council was in full swing,
I took a group of young Brothers—members of my religious
community, an order of lay men devoted to teaching—to wor-

ship with a local pentecostal Church of God congregation at the bottom of the hill from our novitiate in Glencoe, Missouri.

We were initially unnerved by the animation of the worship, used, as we were in those days, only to a prefabricated Latin worship. When the congregation accepted our return invitation to worship with us during the week of prayer for Christian unity, they were wide-eyed at the crucifix and statues in our chapel. (We decided to worship in the music room with piano rather than organ.) Many of these young men continued to visit this pentecostal church and made friends there as part of the spiritual discipline of their novitiate.

One could not imagine in 1965 that by 1970 there would be a full-blown Catholic charismatic movement, that by 1975 there would be a scholarly society with full Catholic and pentecostal participation, that by 1980 there would be a productive dialogue between the Vatican and pentecostals,[17] and that by 1998 the Vatican-pentecostal dialogue would publish a common statement, "Evangelization, Proselytism, and Common Witness."[18]

Pentecostalism is a relatively new movement, having its origins in the Baptist and Holiness-Methodist communities, largely in the South.[19] When Catholics and classical Protestants began to experience this form of spirituality in the late 1960s, many of the same struggles and hopes that emerged in the early pentecostal churches filled this spiritual movement.[20] One of the great gifts of this movement was the level of spiritual communion it created between classical pentecostals and other Christians, including Catholic Christians.[21] For example, from the very beginning more than thirty years ago, the Society for Pentecostal Studies has been a rich forum of theological exploration among Christians of all traditions, providing a true context for ecumenical interchange.[22]

One hopes that high school students who are converted to an appreciation of fellow Christians carry this into adult life. For these young men preparing to be teachers, this experience might mark the beginning of a lifelong interest in building positive relationships among their students from different Christian backgrounds. This conversion and subsequent development has been a great resource for their Christian life.

These formal encounters have been a blessing for me, and, I hope, for the Baptist, pentecostal, Holiness, evangelical, and Catholic Christians who have had the privilege of participating in them. However, given the differences of cultures, the differences of understanding of God's will for the church and its unity, the different methods of evangelization and the tensions these cause in such places as Latin America and Eastern Europe, and the burdens of history, our common Christian faith challenges us even more to deepen our mutual understanding and to find means of common witness to the gospel in the world.

As Pope John Paul II says in his encyclical *Commitment to Unity:*

> If they [believers in Christ] wish truly and effectively to oppose the world's tendency to reduce to powerlessness the mystery of redemption, they must profess together the same truth about the cross. The cross! An anti-Christian outlook seeks to minimize the cross, to empty it of its meaning and to deny that in it man has the source of his new life. It claims that the cross is unable to provide either vision or hope. Man, it says, is nothing but an earthly being, who must live as if God did not exist.[23]

9

Between the Pope and Billy Graham

EVANGELICALS AND CATHOLICS IN DIALOGUE

Timothy George

I have three aims I hope to accomplish in this essay. First, I offer a brief definition of evangelicalism and try to flesh it out a bit. Second, I want to explore the issue of the difficulty of dialogue, or even discussion, between evangelicals and Roman Catholics. Finally, I place the recent discussions of Evangelicals and Catholics Together in the context of an ongoing dialogue by looking, in a cursory way, at some of the documents that have emerged out of the developing relationship between evangelicals and Roman Catholics in recent years.

Evangelicalism: What Is It?

It is not very difficult to define Roman Catholicism. At least, it is rather easy to say what makes one a Roman Catholic. A Roman Catholic is a person affiliated with a church whose bishop is in communion with the Bishop of Rome. That is very straightforward and quite accurate.

There is no such comparable clarity when it comes to defining evangelicalism. We might say with Jerry Falwell that "a fundamentalist is just an evangelical who is mad at somebody!"

Or we might listen to Dr. Bob Jones, Sr., who once said that an evangelical is someone who says to a liberal, "I'll call you a Christian if you'll call me a scholar!" There is a measure of truth, as well as humor, in both definitions.

More seriously, David Bebbington has identified four basic characteristics of evangelicalism. Evangelicals of all stripes, he says, stress the importance of personal conversion to Christ, an activist approach to evangelism and promotion of the faith, a high view of the Bible, and the centrality of the cross. "All those who display conversionism, activism, biblicism, and crucicentrism are evangelicals."[1] Bebbington's evangelical quadrilateral has gained credence as a helpful summary of the essence of the evangelical faith.

However, I suggest a simpler and even briefer definition: *evangelicalism is a renewal movement within historic Christian orthodoxy.* Its theology and piety have been enriched by many diverse tributaries, including Puritanism, pietism, and Pentecostalism, but its sense of identity as a distinctive faith community, what we might call the *evangelical tradition,* has been shaped decisively by three major episodes: the Protestant Reformation, the evangelical Awakening, and the fundamentalist-modernist controversy.

The Reformers of the sixteenth century rediscovered a theology of grace that had been obscured, though not completely lost, in the medieval church. They wanted to reorder that church on the basis of the Holy Scriptures, God's Word written. Though they differed among themselves on many issues, the Reformers held fast to what later became known as the material and formal principles of the Reformation: justification by faith alone and the sufficiency of the Bible as the normative rule of belief and practice.

The evangelical Awakening of the eighteenth century was a great movement of God's Spirit led by John and Charles Wesley, George Whitefield, and Jonathan Edwards, among others. Much of what we associate with later evangelicalism comes from this period: hymn singing, mass evangelism, the modern missionary movement, Bible societies, Christian social reform, and so on. All of these were controversial at the time, not unlike today's intra-evangelical debates over worship styles and strategies for church growth.

At the dawn of the twentieth century, the evangelical consensus shaped by the Reformation and the Awakening was
threatened by theological liberalism and the rise of destructive
biblical criticism. This led to fierce debates and church splits
between fundamentalist defenders of the faith and their ac-
commodationist critics. After World War II, a new coalition of
post-fundamentalist evangelicals emerged. These "neo-evangelicals" believed as firmly as the fundamentalists in the truth-
fulness of the Bible, but they also believed Christians should be
intellectually strong, culturally literate, socially engaged, and
cooperative in spirit. Blessed with visionary leaders such as
Billy Graham, John Stott, Carl Henry, and Bill Bright, evangelicals in the past half-century have moved from the margins into
the mainstream, with a proliferation of publications, institutions, and parachurch ministries.

Evangelicals are united with all orthodox Christians on such
key doctrines of the faith as the Holy Trinity and the classic
christology of the early church. Fundamentalism ignored (although it assumed) this great dogmatic tradition in the name of
simple biblicism, while liberalism denied (or at least downplayed) it in the interest of cultural relevance. Evangelicals
gladly celebrate these doctrines as essential to the gospel itself.
But we also believe these teachings have important implications for how we work, worship, pray, order our families, and
relate to the world around us.

An evangelical is a herald charged to deliver an urgent message. Many things can be said about a herald, but what matters
most is the message he or she is charged to deliver. The word
we bring is the greatest news ever spoken or heard. Evangelicals are people with passion to know the living God—the Father, the Son, and the Holy Spirit—and to make his grace and
love known to every person on earth.

The Difficulty of Dialogue

Why has it been so difficult for evangelicals, especially those in
North America, to enter into meaningful dialogue with Roman
Catholics? First, American Protestants in general, and evangelicals in particular, have been deeply influenced by a virulent
strain of nativism that is deeply embedded in the history of our

country. The rise of the Know-Nothing party in the nineteenth century, and the spread of the Ku Klux Klan in the early twentieth century, are only two of the more visible indicators of this phenomenon. The first presidential election I can remember with any clarity was the contest between Richard Nixon and John F. Kennedy in 1960. Although my father, like most good Southerners in those days, always voted Democratic, I remember his being greatly agitated at the prospect of a Catholic in the White House. If Kennedy were elected President, it was said, it would not be long before the United States of America would become a fiefdom of the Church of Rome. The national security of the country would be jeopardized since the president would owe a deeper loyalty to the pope than to his own country and would doubtless be constantly on the phone to Rome seeking papal advice on every decision of state. One of the turning points in that campaign was Kennedy's address to Southern Baptist ministers in Houston seeking to assuage such fears. As it turned out, there was not very much to worry about, not least because Kennedy was not such a good Catholic to start with and certainly not ultramontanist in his approach to religion and politics. The kind of anti-Catholic rhetoric heard in the 1960 presidential campaign is far more subdued within the evangelical subculture today, but it is not completely absent. In subtle and sometimes overt ways, it continues to shape fundamentalist and evangelical perceptions of Roman Catholics.

Second, the long history of deep-seated antipathy and hostility between Catholics and Protestants stemming from the Reformation era has yet to be overcome. The scars of religious wars, the centuries of hatred, bitterness, separation, isolation, and mutual recrimination have become deeply lodged in the collective memories of the two communities.

I shall never forget my first visit to Cambridge, England, several years ago. Near one of the common greens in that city stands the Church of the English Martyrs. On a beautiful sunny afternoon, I sauntered into that church, not really noticing where I was going, thinking to myself that this must be a church dedicated to the memory of Cranmer, Ridley, Hooper, the great martyrs of John Foxe's *Acts and Monuments*. In fact, to my surprise, it turned out to be a Roman Catholic church dedicated to the memory of recusant martyrs, that is, Catholics who were loyal to Rome and hence faced persecution and sometimes death at the hands of the Protestant magistracy. Both sides have their horror stories to remember and recount. We have yet to achieve a reconciliation of shared memories between our two communities, and this makes it difficult to sit down and talk about our commonalities in Christ.

A third reason why it is difficult for evangelicals to talk to Roman Catholics is the continuing tradition of apocalypticism in which the Roman Catholic Church and the pope are assumed to play a very definite role. In many popular evangelical understandings of eschatology, the harlot of the Book of Revelation is equated directly with the Church of Rome or the pope. This line of interpretation is deeply rooted in the Protestant heritage and has re-surfaced with a vengeance in recent decades, along with the explosion of popular interest in the details of the end time reflected in numerous best-selling books from Hal Lindsey's *Late Great Planet Earth* to the Left Behind series.

And then, fourth, as other essays in this volume have shown, among many evangelicals and fundamentalists, ecumenical ventures of any kind are greeted with deep suspicion. Many evangelicals find it difficult to imagine that serious discussion and conversation with Roman Catholics about fundamental theological issues could be done without compromising the essential tenets of the Reformation. Some of the most severe critics of ECT are those who want to preserve at all costs the distinctive emphases of the sixteenth-century Reformers. Frequently enough, they have little appreciation for the true ecumenical intentions and efforts of the Reformers themselves. Both Luther and Calvin saw the Reformation as a tragic necessity. Some of their latter-day champions appreciate the necessity but fail to discern the tragic element in that great rupture. At the same time, there is often a lack of appreciation for the development of doctrine within Roman Catholic theology. While the whole complex of issues related to the relative authority of Scripture, tradition, and the magisterial teaching office presents enormous problems for Roman Catholic and evangelical dialogue, to imagine that nothing has changed within Roman Catholicism since the Council of Trent is to be historically naive if not willfully ignorant. It should be said that the fear of compromising the true faith through interconfessional dialogue is not limited to evangelicals. Certain Roman Catholic critics of ECT have leveled a similar charge against our Roman Catholic interlocutors who seem to them to have given away the shop by signing on to Protestant-sounding language, including the affirmation of justification by faith alone.

Review of Documents

For most of the past century, evangelicals and Roman Catholics have stood not only in opposition to one another but also in isolation from one another. In 1928, Pope Pius XI issued his encyclical *Mortalium animos* in which he stated "the unity of Christians can come about only by furthering the return to the one true church of Christ of those who are separated from it."[2] A sea change in Catholic ecumenism occurred on January 26, 1959, when Pope John XXIII announced that he intended to call an ecumenical council to deal, among other things, with the issue of Christian unity. The decrees of the Second Vatican Council, especially the Dogmatic Constitution on the Church (*Lumen Gentium*) and the Decree on Ecumenism (*Unitatis Redintegratio*), both promulgated on November 21, 1964, opened a new chapter in the history of ecumenical engagement which continues to this day under the guidance of the Pontifical Council for Promoting Christian Unity.

Many of the themes set forth in the documents of Vatican II are picked up and further developed in *Ut Unum Sint* (That All May Be One), the landmark ecumenical encyclical released by Pope John Paul II on May 30, 1995.[3] This document both underscores the importance of interconfessional dialogue and calls for ongoing practical cooperation among Christians who are ecclesially separated from one another. This document is also marked by an unstinted commitment to the indispensability of truth as the basis for true Christian unity. Interlaced throughout *Ut Unum Sint* is this constant theme reiterated by Pope John Paul II: "Love for the truth is the deepest dimension of any authentic quest for full communion between Chris-

tians. . . . The unity willed by God can be obtained only by the
adherence of all to the content of revealed faith in its entirety
in matters of faith; compromise is in contradiction with God,
who is Truth. In the body of Christ, 'the Way, and the Truth,
and the Life' (John 14:6), who could consider legitimate a reconciliation brought about at the expense of the truth?"[4]
   One reason why most evangelicals have stood aloof from
modern ecumenical efforts supervised by mainline Protestants
is a perceived lack of the kind of passionate quest for truth
which resonates throughout *Ut Unum Sint*. Thus, in review-
ing ecumenical efforts of the past three decades, Konrad Raiser,
secretary-general of the World Council of Churches, called for
an "urgent reordering of the ecumenical agenda away from old
doctrinal disputes and unresolvable arguments of the past toward more urgent contemporary issues such as justice, peace,
and concern for the environment."[5] No doubt such an agenda
fits in well with postmodernist notions of truth and the reign-
ing ideology of pluralism which dominate the declining world
of mainline Protestant enterprises. But it falls immeasurably
short of the apostolic mandate to speak the truth in love. On
this point, evangelicals can offer a hearty "Amen!" to these
words of Cardinal Joseph Ratzinger: "Our quarreling ancestors
were in reality much closer to each other when in all their disputes they still knew that they could only be servants of one
truth which must be acknowledged as being as great and as
pure as it has been intended for us by God."[6]
   While it must be acknowledged that most evangelicals are
much less involved in ecumenical discussions than the Roman
Catholic Church, there is a growing body of evangelical literature that reflects a serious theological engagement with Roman
Catholics. One of the earliest, and most important, of these en-
gagements was the Evangelical-Roman Catholic Dialogue on
Mission (ERCDOM), a report that emerged from a series of
three meetings which took place over a period of seven years
from 1977 through 1984, with consultations held in France,
Italy, and England. The final ERCDOM report was edited by
Basil Meeking and John Stott. It purported to be in no sense an
"agreed statement," but rather a faithful record of the discussions and ideas shared in the conversations. In addition to John
Stott, the evangelical participants included Orlando Costas,

David Hubbard, David Wells, and Peter Beyerhaus. The following issues were addressed in the report: "Revelation and Authority," "The Nature of Mission," "The Gospel of Salvation," "Our Response in the Holy Spirit to the Gospel," "The Church and the Gospel," "The Gospel and Culture," and the "Possibilities of Common Witness." There is also a brief section on "The Role of Mary in Salvation." Many of these themes have since been taken up in the ongoing ECT process.

ERCDOM was preoccupied with the overarching issue of mission, an appropriate theme for Roman Catholic–evangelical discussion. We might say that what ecumenism is to Roman Catholicism, mission (or missions, to use the preferred term of most conservative Protestants) is to evangelicalism—the indispensable imperative of Christian faith and churchly life. ERCDOM also set forth two dialogical principles that would be later extended in the ECT process. First, it was recognized that the most fruitful kind of evangelical–Roman Catholic engagement would likely rise out of joint Bible study, as both sides regarded the Bible as God's Word and acknowledged the need to read, study, believe, and obey it. Second, ERCDOM hints at the emerging alliance between Roman Catholics and evangelicals on "the great theological and ethical issues which are being debated in all the churches." This statement presaged what I would later call in a *Christianity Today* editorial an "ecumenism of the trenches."[7]

Roughly contemporary with the ERCDOM process was another initiative sponsored by the World Evangelical Fellowship (WEF; now known as the World Evangelical Association), a loose-knit global coalition of more than fifty autonomous national and regional bodies of conservative evangelical Christians. In 1980, Waldron Scott, general secretary of WEF, invited two Roman Catholic observers, Ralph Martin and Basil Meeking, to attend the WEF General Assembly in Hoddesdon, England. This incident created a minor furor within WEF circles, resulting in an apology by General Secretary Scott and the appointment of an Ecumenical Issues Task Force charged with studying the relationship between evangelicalism and Roman Catholicism.[8] Noting "the many facets of change in Roman Catholic position and policy," and the "many different faces of Rome . . . manifested in different parts of the world," the task force prepared a lengthy statement setting forth evangelical convictions on many controverted issues such as the authority of the church, the pope and infallibility, justification by faith alone, sacramentalism and the Eucharist, the place of Mary, and the mission of the church. While rejoicing that the former hard line of the Church of Rome against non-Catholic Christians had been relaxed by Vatican II, the document declared frankly that evangelicals "are not prepared" to accept the claim that "the Church of Rome is the only true church, nor that its supreme teaching office is free from all error in matters of belief, nor that the road that leads to Rome is the way to unity."[9]

The Eighth General Assembly of WEF overwhelmingly approved the document as presented by the task force in June 1986. While the WEF document has been characterized as a "relatively negative statement on Roman Catholicism," it is important to recognize that the statement does express appreciation for "the willingness of the Church of Rome to enter into discussion with theologians of various confessions on equal basis" and also expresses hope that further dialogue can be undertaken.[10]

One further note concerning the WEF process: some of the deepest misgivings concerning evangelical-Catholic rapprochement have been expressed by evangelical leaders in countries such as Italy, Spain, and others in Latin America where Catholicism is the dominant tradition. It is important for evangelicals engaged in dialogue with Roman Catholics in North America to remember that some of their evangelical brothers and sisters in other parts of the world may lack enthusiasm for what they consider "armchair ecumenism" due to their own indigenous experience of isolation, hostility, and even persecution. Such evangelical critics, however resistant and reactionary their views may seem, cannot be omitted from any true consideration of catholicity.

Before turning to the ECT documents, I must mention the remarkable series of dialogues between the Roman Catholic Church and some classical pentecostal churches and leaders. These discussions began even earlier than the ERCDOM process, starting in 1972 when Vatican II was still a very fresh memory, having concluded its final session in 1965. For more than thirty years, Roman Catholic and pentecostal church leaders have pursued a number of themes and produced a series of documents, perhaps the most significant of which is "Evangelization, Common Witness, and Proselytism" (1994). While the pentecostal–Roman Catholic dialogue had no official link to the ECT process, both initiatives have shared a common concern for growing conflict between evangelicals and Roman Catholics in many places in the world, including, perhaps most urgently, Latin America. The pentecostal–Roman Catholic dialogue has recognized the difficulty of a common witness in situations of conflict (and even violence) between the two faith communities and has tried to distinguish a proper gospel witness from proselytizing efforts that use underhanded and unethical means. In such discussions, it is important to recognize that abuses of civility and Christian charity have occurred on both/all sides and that all who claim the name of Christ are bound by his Gospel mandate in John 13:34–35: "I give you a new commandment: Love one another; as I have loved you, so you are to love one another. If there is this love among you, then all will know that you are my disciples" (NEB).

Not since the publication of the Chicago Statement on Biblical Inerrancy (1978) has any document stirred so many hornets within the evangelical nest as "Evangelicals and Catholics Together: Christian Mission in the Third Millennium" (1994). ECT I, as this document came to be called, was produced by a group of Roman Catholic and evangelical theologians convened by Chuck Colson and Richard John Neuhaus. This document frankly recognized a litany of social and cultural concerns shared by Roman Catholics and evangelicals alike, issues such as the sanctity of human life, the spread of pornography, the evacuation of moral decision making in public life, and patterns of dehumanization which increasingly mark what Pope John Paul II has called "the culture of death."

Some critics of ECT I dismissed it as a social or political manifesto produced by conservative Christians who had put aside their theological differences in order to enter into a coalition of convenience. However, ECT I did address, albeit in a cursory way, important theological issues, and it also called for a continuing process of study, discussion, and prayer—"for a better understanding of one another's convictions and a more adequate comprehension of the truth of God in Christ." Perhaps the most significant advance made by ECT I was the frank recognition that faithful evangelicals and believing Roman Catholics could and should refer openly to one another as "brothers and sisters in Christ." While some evangelicals were happy to support Roman Catholic–evangelical co-belligerency on matters of social and cultural concern, they were strongly resistant to any efforts toward a shared theological understanding.

However, in 1997, a second ECT document was published, "The Gift of Salvation."[11] To some extent, "The Gift of Salvation" was a response to two important topics of perceived ambiguity in the earlier ECT statement: the doctrine of justification by faith alone and the biblical mandate for world missions and world evangelization. "The Gift of Salvation" declared that justification was not earned by any good works or merits of our own, that it was entirely God's gift. Further, this document stated that "in justification, God, on the basis of Christ's righteousness alone, declares us to be no longer his rebellious enemies but his forgiven friends, and by virtue of his declaration it is so. . . . We understand that what we here affirm is in agreement with what the Reformation traditions have meant by justification by faith alone (*sola fide*)." These two sentences elicited numerous responses of surprise and even shock that evangelical and Roman Catholic theologians could affirm such things together. At the same time, the document honestly noted that, despite this remarkable convergence, significant differences still remained: "While we rejoice in the unity we have discovered and are confident of the fundamental truths about the gift of salvation we have affirmed, we recognize that there are necessarily interrelated questions that require further and urgent exploration. . . . We are committed to examining these questions further in our continuing conversations."

Those discussions led, in the next round of ECT meetings, to a fresh examination of the controverted relationship between Scripture and tradition. Historically, this issue has been framed in terms of a fundamental difference on the very source of Christian teaching. Is that teaching based on Scripture alone (*sola Scriptura*), on the one hand, or Scripture and authoritative tradition, on the other? In a document entitled "Your Word Is Truth" (ECT III), the Catholic and evangelical interlocutors recognized persistent differences in their views of the church, the scope of the biblical canon, and both the shape and jurisdictional authority of the magisterial office in the church. However, in a key passage, the framers of this document were able to break through to an important consensus:

> Together we affirm that Scripture is the divinely inspired and uniquely authoritative written revelation of God; as such it is normative for the teaching and life of the church. We also affirm that tradition, rightly understood as the proper reflection of biblical teaching, is the faithful transmission of the truth of the Gospel from generation to generation through the power of the Holy Spirit. As evangelicals and Catholics fully committed to our respective heritages, we affirm together the coinherence of Scripture and tradition: tradition is not a second source of revelation alongside the Bible but must ever be corrected and informed by it, and Scripture itself is not understood in a vacuum apart from the historical existence in life of the community of faith. Faithful believers in every generation live by the memories and hopes of the *actus tradendi* of the Holy Spirit. This is true whenever and wherever the Word of God is faithfully translated, sincerely believed, and truly preached.

This document also referred to the Holy Spirit as "the Supreme Magisterium of God" (a phrase supplied by J. I. Packer, one of the ECT signatories), and concluded by affirming together "those foundational truths of historic Christian orthodoxy that we do share in common" while invoking the Holy Spirit's continuing guidance for further establishing and making manifest "our unity in the truth of Jesus Christ, so that the world may come to believe" (John 17:21).[12] It would be too much to say that "Your Word Is Truth" has mended the historic rift between evangelicals and Catholics on the basic question of religious authority. But, as Charles Colson and Richard John Neuhaus say in their introduction to the volume of essays gathered around this ECT statement, "We believe the statement does go a long way toward recasting an old dispute in a new and promising way. It underscores the utter singularity of the authority of Scripture and, at the same time, the unavoidable necessity of discerning the right interpretation of Scripture in the history of Christian faith and life—a history that is rightly called tradition."[13] "Your Word Is Truth" comes at a time when evangelicals are showing a renewed and growing interest in the history of biblical exegesis, the issue of doctrinal development, and the ecumenical context of spiritual theology. The ECT project has moved forward with a new statement, "The Communion of Saints," released in 2003, and the subject of the Christian life has been taken up in a new series of discussions on "the universal call to holiness."

Conclusion

Several years ago, Wolfhart Pannenberg looked forward into the twenty-first century and declared that, as he saw it, the three vibrant forces within the world Christian movement for the foreseeable future would be Orthodoxy, Roman Catholicism, and evangelical Protestantism. While the century is still young, there is every reason to think that Pannenberg's prediction was on target. Orthodoxy, for all its strength, remains more or less confined to defined ethnic and regional strongholds. The two universalizing and aggressively missionary families within the Christian movement are Catholics and evangelicals. For this reason alone, the documents we have surveyed in this essay, and the various dialogues that have produced them, are signposts for an emerging ecumenical phalanx that will surely be far more prominent at the end of this century than at its beginning. For faithful evangelicals and believing Roman Catholics, this is a time to sew, not a time to rend. In expressing our common convictions about Christian faith and mission, we can do no better than to heed the words of John Calvin: "That we acknowledge no unity except in Christ; no charity of which he is not the bond, and that, therefore, the chief point in preserving charity is to maintain faith sacred and entire."

Part 5

EVANGELICALS
AND ECUMENISM

10

Ecumenical and Evangelical

MUTUAL AFFIRMATION AND ADMONITION

Gabriel Fackre

What is an "ecumenical perspective"? Or to turn it into a noun parallel to the noun *evangelical,* what is an *ecumenical*? My understanding of these things grows out of participation in the twentieth-century pilgrimage toward church unity called the ecumenical movement.[1]

A little personal history. The meaning of the word *ecumenical* began to take shape when my wife and I, as theological students, hitchhiked across Europe to attend the first meeting of the World Council of Churches in Amsterdam in 1948. It was further formed while serving as a pastor, then as a teacher, in the United Church of Christ (UCC), the first and as yet only attempt in this country at organic church union of diverse Protestant traditions—Reformed, evangelical, Congregational, Christian. It was honed by involvement in the Consultation on Church Union, a movement toward merger of nine denominations that began in 1962, but then scaled back in the 1980s toward a less ambitious goal of "covenant," which in January 2002 created a new body of thirty million Christians in the United States called Churches Uniting in Christ, made up of a range of communions from African American churches to Presbyterian, Methodist, Episcopal, UCC, and other denominations.[2] This ecumenical shaping continued as part of a Reformed-Lutheran team of theologians that helped lay the groundwork for the 1997 "full communion" agreement among four Lutheran and Reformed bodies in this country. And as a Reformed theologian I have been much in dialogue with Roman Catholics and Lutherans on their recent joint declaration on the doctrine of justification.[3]

Historically, a strong impetus for this form of ecumenism—conciliar, bilateral, multilateral—came from within the old-line denominations and traditions stemming from the Reformation. Now the word *ecumenical* describes a move toward unity more far-reaching, including Eastern Orthodox, Roman Catholic, pentecostal, and other traditions. I confine myself in these remarks mostly to the old-line church progenitors of the twentieth-century movement. These constituencies in this country and in Europe have many problems, to which I will allude, needing, among other things, admonitions from evangelicals. But they do have a long and hard-won history of ecumenical witness to the gospel, rooted ultimately in Christ's own prayer to the Father, "that they may be one as we are one" (John 17:22). I stand squarely on that soil. And I do so as an adjectival ecumenical, an *evangelical* ecumenical, committed to evangelical centralities, and with an eye on convergences and a hope for alliances.[4]

One of the formulas current in ecumenical circles is "mutual affirmation and admonition." The phrase was put in circulation by the North American Lutheran-Reformed conversation,[5] and is commended by ecumenist Harding Myer as a fresh way of proceeding on the path toward Christian unity.[6] I see it as an extension of the Pauline counsel to the Corinthian church rent by factionalism: "The eye cannot say to the hand. 'I have no need of you . . .'" (1 Cor. 12:21). Surely Paul's declaration to that congregation is close to the premise of this conference. Philip Yancey struck just that note in a recent column in *Christianity Today*, "Fixing Our Weakest Link," asserting that "Evangelicals should be more 'needful of the minds of others.'"[7] A grasp of the *full* gospel grows finally out of a *whole* body. When evangelicals invite others into the conversation, there is hope for the healing of our somatic brokenness. In that spirit of mutual edification, I will speak about common ecumenical-evangelical affirmations, then ecumenical admonition of evangelicals, and finally evangelical admonition of ecumenicals.

Ecumenical-Evangelical Affirmations

What made the recent Lutheran–Roman Catholic joint declaration on justification possible was a thirty-five-year dialogue that identified a convergence on core teaching, along with the honest recognition of divergence in accents and interpretations.[8] The same was true in decades of study that eventuated in official Lutheran-Reformed agreements, national and international.[9] My guess is that there is a mutual affirmation regarding certain basics in this gathering with the five conversation partners sharing enough of the fundaments to warrant this respectful exchange.[10] As our purpose here is to attend to, and learn from, one another's differences, I make only passing reference to these commonalities. Surely they have to do, for one, with matters of authority, as in the primacy of Scripture and the importance of Christian tradition in the interpretation of Scripture. And they also extend to the specifics of doctrine, with the classical teaching on the Trinity and the person of Christ; newly asserted convergences on the redemptive work of Christ, accomplished and applied;[11] the witness to the "supernatural," and to the transcendent dimension (contra Enlightenment premises) on matters that run from the human beings both made in the image of God and fallen, through biblical miracles to the reality of the resurrection; a broadly agreed understanding of the church as a gathering of the faithful around Word and sacrament/ordinance; and a shared conviction about the last chapter of the Christian story, an expectation of the resurrection of the dead, the return of Christ, the final judgment, and life everlasting in the final reign of God (the creedal refrains). We stand together on these first principles, confronting modernity and postmodernity with this alternative view of the world and the world to come. Perhaps, too, the current crisis has sharpened our sense of shared Christian basics when compared to other religious worldviews. I could not help but think of the difference between the bin Laden version of Muslim faith (repudiated by much of the Islamic world itself) that holds suicide bombing to be a passport to paradise, and a Christian eschatology that believes the perpetrators of such will face instead the wrath of a righteous God. Commonalities in Christian doctrine make possible a mutual affirmation that, in turn, facilitates an honest exchange on the differences in the accents and interpretations of the gospel. Is it possible that such can be an occasion for mutual learning, and for developing a richer and more powerful shared witness to our time and place? On then to the mutual admonitions that might be catalysts for this kind of two-way fructification. But first, the more detailed ecumenical admonitory perspective on evangelicalism.

Ecumenical Admonitions

Worldly Evangelicals

Beware the hand of Jehu! You remember the incident in 2 Kings 10:16 when this king invites the prophet Jehonadab up into his chariot, "Come with me and see my zeal for the Lord." But Jehu was on his way to Samaria to kill the remaining members of the royal family, and was looking for religious cover from Jehonadab. Proximity to power can be seductive, even for prophets.

We saw a rerun of this chariot trip several years ago. Clergy, including prominent evangelical figures, were invited to presidential prayer breakfasts and into close White House associations, eventuating in applause and apologias for President Clinton's professed penitence. A group of critics, in their volume *Judgment Day at the White House,* read these events as the political manipulation of naive religionists, giving Marxists ammunition for their charge that piety is just a smokescreen for privilege.[12]

Must evangelicals be especially wary of these seductions? A consultation several years ago posed this question with the widely reported Bill Hybels/Bill Clinton softball exchange as background, and members of the Willow Creek staff on hand.[13] Warnings *are* in order, for the same temptations are possible, perhaps even more so, with the Bush administration and its kinship with evangelical concerns and friendships with its leaders.

Ecumenical admonition of evangelicals draws here on its ecumenical old-line church lineage of proximity to power. Its "establishment" history, in the distant past and up to the 1950s in this country, often found it hand in glove with the principalities and powers. As old-line churches become increasingly marginal, they awaken more and more to their embarrassing record of cultural captivity, and begin to talk of themselves as "resident aliens."[14] Of course, this posture has its own dangers, a sectarian self-righteousness. However, a history of being manipulated by power brings a sobriety that has lessons for others. To "new-line" evangelicals with their growing proximity to centers of power, the old-line will say, "Been there, done that, so be careful. Beware the hand of Jehu!"

There are theological as well as historical issues here. At their best, on some occasions, the old-line churches did say a bold "No!" to their seducers—at least a remnant within them did so. Think of the Confessing Church in Germany in the 1930s with the leadership given by a Karl Barth or Dietrich Bonhoeffer, and of its Barmen Declaration:

> Jesus Christ, as he is attested for us in Holy Scripture, is the one Word of God which we have to hear and which we have to trust and obey in life and in death. . . . We reject the false doctrine that the Church were permitted to abandon the form of its message . . . to changes in prevailing ideological and political convictions.[15]

What saves the ecumenical old-line from cultural captivity on such occasions is a bold Christocentricity juxtaposed to an anthropocentricity, which makes our experiences—political, ideological, or religious—the defining characteristic of faith. Barmen's stress on Christ as the "one Word" has since found its way into more than a few ecumenical and denominational charters. Here we take note of this learning that the one Word, Jesus Christ, must be our pole star, not our feelings, philosophies, and ideologies.

The "world" has its attractions for evangelicals in academia as well as politics. I remember vividly an occasion at the American Academy of Religion, a section meeting in which religious pluralist Paul Knitter was holding forth, with a prominent evangelical theologian making a fawning response devoid of the hard-hitting commitment to particularity one would expect. At another meeting an evangelical panel was asked to respond to the year's headliner, Jürgen Moltmann. Again, it appeared that the panelists were so taken with being in the presence of the mighty that critical words were scarcely heard.

Can these incidents be traced to "the open view of God" currently popular in some evangelical quarters? I have said so in a critical review of the view's defenders in their volumes, *The Openness of God* and *Unbounded Love*.[16] Excited evangelicals making what they think are new discoveries of "megashift" proportions overlook that old-line theology has already tread the inviting path of openness, tender love, the divine immanence, creativity. . . . We had to hear from a Karl Barth or Reinhold Niebuhr a sharp rebuke for forgetting the need for biblical *closure, tough* love, the divine *transcendence,* and recognition of the persistence of *sin* in the most creative advances. Evangelicalism, achieving new prominence, can go the way of an earlier mainline theology, running the risks of courting the cultural establishment and muting its No! to the powers and principalities.

Convertive Piety and Its Problems

A "convertive piety," as Stanley Grenz describes it,[17] marks evangelicalism. Thank God for this witness to personal salvation, a word the wider church needs to hear, as I shall presently argue. But there is also a danger in the stress on individual appropriation and feeling-drenched spirituality. For one, it invites the believer to think in anthropocentric terms. For another it can reduce the importance of the corporate dimension of the gospel. And for another, it can result in an un-self-critical us-and-them mentality. Let's look at each of these vulnerabilities.

Karl Barth was deeply appreciative of evangelical piety, as in his tribute to Abel Burkhardt.[18] However, he also saw the dangers inherent in a subjectivity that becomes definitive of the gospel.

> It was an intolerable truncation of the Christian message when the older Protestantism steered the whole doctrine of the atonement—and with it, ultimately the whole of theology into the *cul de sac* of the individual experience of grace. . . . The result was that the great concepts of justifica-

tion and sanctification came more and more to be understood
and filled out psychologically and biographically. . . .[19]

To the extent that what *we* do or feel or think becomes the
focus of our faith, as in our personal "born-again" experience,
we have moved, anthropocentrically, away from the proper
focus of our faith: the triune God. Our human subjectivity becomes the measure of the divine objectivity. One can hear the
echoes of this in the kind of gospel song that gives pride of
place to "I, me, and mine," telling *my* story rather than *God's*
story.[20] Barth is known for his attack on Schleiermacher's feel-
ing-oriented anthropocentricity and therefore kept a sharp eye
out for inordinate claims for *our* religious experience, whether
evangelical piety or the nineteenth-century romantic spirituality. In both cases he saw the danger of God's one Word, Jesus
Christ, as attested by Scripture, being displaced. Barth's alternative has its own problems, of course, the danger being to di-
minish the salvific weight of personal faith in the pilgrimage,
all humanity being, in principle, redeemed on Calvary, the "in
fact" left up to a final divine decision (short of the "universal-
ism" of which Barth is regularly charged).[21] How to see the
evangelical experience as *ministerial* and not *magisterial* is the
challenge of evangelical-ecumenical mutual learning.[22]

Again, the individualism to which evangelical piety is prey
can so stress *personal* choice that the ecclesial environs which
it inhabits, and the sacramental means of grace integral to such
piety, are not given their due. In my own Reformed tradition
the impact of eighteenth- and nineteenth-century revivalism,
while bringing to the fore the needed place for personal decision, eroded the catechetical and sacramental aspects of that
tradition. A corrective appeared in the "Mercersburg theology"
of John Williamson Nevin and Philip Schaff that challenged
pietist reductionism with its churchly theology. One sees the
same Mercersburg instinct on the current scene in the phenomenon of evangelicals on the "road" to Constantinople or
Rome. In contrast to these, however, the Mercersburg movement (still very much alive today) insisted upon both the formal and material principles of Protestantism,[23] so expressed in
its famous fighting word, "*evangelical* catholicity."

Again a convertive piety stressing the boundary line of a

"born-again" experience invites an us-and-them mentality. This we-they juxtaposition makes for the passionate evangelism of evangelicals, a determination to get out the Word that calls for the decision of faith, one that puts to shame inarticulate and unmotivated old-liners. It contributes as well to the zeal of evangelicals when they enter the political arena, carrying with it the assumption that politics is a battle between the armies of light and the legions of night. However, in both cases, the us-versus-them juxtaposition makes for a mentality that fails to see the sin that persists in the champions of the truth as well as its foes, and eventuates in an off-putting self-righteous fury. In politics in a democracy, where effectiveness is the art of the possible, not the perfect, such a juxtaposition militates against the necessary building of coalitions, a lesson of which the perfectionist is innocent.

In the life of the Spirit, a graphic example of the absence of self-realism and self-criticism was apparent in the fall of the evangelical television titans in the 1980s. "Money, sex, and power!" the media trumpeted as the Bakers, Swaggart, and others succumbed to their blandishments.[24] When the new birth is construed as a watershed cleansing, sin therefore being essentially the problem of others—the unrescued—the saved are presumed invulnerable to temptation. We found out otherwise.

In historic Reformation traditions as continued in old-line ecumenical churches there is a sensibility about sin built into the liturgical life through a regularized public confession of sin. It appears in almost all of these churches' official services for the Lord's Day and all of their services of Word and sacrament. *Simul iustus et peccator!* . . . at the same time righteous and sinner. When such is part of the ethos of piety, believers are regularly reminded that they are not exempt from the assaults to which a fallen world is prey. What would a theology of *simul iustus et peccator* and a piety of regular public, or even personal, confession do for evangelicals who may be tempted to think that the new birth insulates them from the world, the flesh, and the devil?

Evangelicalism and Excluded Constituencies

In research I did recently for an article on the state of theology today,[25] I came to the section on evangelical women theologians and asked Gordon-Conwell's Catherine Clark Kroeger, now editing the *InterVarsity Women's Bible Commentary* and drawing on those resources, "Who are the women evangelical theologians comparable to feminist movers and shakers Rosemary Radford Ruether, Mary Daly, Letty Russell, Elisabeth Shüssler Fiorenza, Susan Brooks Thistlethwaite . . . ?" Her answer: while there are some mid-career and older evangelical women beginning to have widespread impact, there are none comparable in influence to the foregoing. "Why?" I asked. Answer: Evangelical women were excluded from the educational resources for developing their talents and had no comparable opportunities in the culture of evangelicalism. However, she then began to list an array of younger scholars, mostly with no name recognition, now given the educational opportunities denied to their forebears, making their voices heard. Surely there are grounds for admonition here. The absence of opportunity and the earlier reluctance of the evangelical establishment to welcome women into theological leadership has meant that the needed evangelical women's theological counterpoint to ideological religious feminism is weakened. Male voices are aplenty, of course. But this critical dialogue needs to be carried on first and foremost by women, if the large and growing generation of women entering service to the church is to hear a bold and articulate counterword to current ideology.

In preparation for the same survey, I asked the same question of Hispanic and African American evangelical colleagues in academia about ethnic evangelical theologians who might be considered peers, or peers-to-be, of a Gustavo Gutiérrez or a James Cone. Answer: ethnic evangelicals tend to identify themselves less as "evangelical" and more in terms of their tradition or their ethnicity. If this is true, it is worth asking, Why? Has "evangelical" been so closely associated with white, Euro/North American exponents that ethnic theologians who share the marks of both evangelical doctrine and evangelical piety decline to associate themselves with the self-identified evangelical community? Admonition cuts both ways here, for ecumenical theology and culture have a similar difficulty in drawing ethnic colleagues into their ranks and relationships.

There is a theological premise here that accounts for ecumenical/old-line early outreach to women and ethnic constituencies, and that is the incorporation of "world" in its authority structure as catalyst for rereading Scripture and tradition in the light of questions posed by context and contemporaneity. At its best, a doctrine of common grace, or Barth's "free communications" and "parables of the kingdom"[26] or the like, keeps the ecumenical impulse attentive to cultural developments, as in the protest movements of the nineteenth and twentieth centuries that prompted the reach toward the marginalized. Within Scripture there are rich resources for evangelicals to see that God is not without a witness in the world beyond the church (Acts 14:17), one that may even use an Assyria as the rod of the divine wrath against the chosen people (Isa. 10:5).

Evangelical Separatism

Surely there were evangelicals at the 1948 founding meeting of the World Council of Churches. But they were not the architects of twentieth-century ecumenism in any of its expressions—old-line Protestant, Eastern Orthodox, Roman Catholic, or official combinations thereof. Yes, there is evidence of more recent efforts, self-conscious and helpful presence at World Council assemblies, unofficial efforts such as Evangelicals and Catholics Together, and, of course, an intra-evangelical ecumenism in such bodies as the National Association of Evangelicals. But during the rise of the ecumenical movement as it is customarily understood, there has been a marked wariness by evangelicals of affiliations, dialogues, and binding ecumenical agreements. We shall examine the reasons for this caution, but, for now, let's put the shoe on the other foot: Evangelicals deny to ecumenism the gift evangelicals could bring to the wider body of Christ. And evangelicals impoverish their own understanding of the gospel when they stand aside from the ecumenical movement.

On the first count, evangelicalism is a vital part of the church catholic, sharing its baptismal unity and commitment to classical core convictions. Further, its firm stand on the authority of Scripture and its devotional use, and its witness to the existential appropriation of justifying faith, are desperately needed charisms in a wider church. As the first is already true and the second is a Pauline imperative, it is wrong when evangelicals circle their wagons and treat the ecumenical movement as an advancing enemy. Let them be what they are and bring their gift to the rest of us.

On the second count, evangelical separatism denies to itself learnings about aspects of the gospel which can only come from close association with other parts of the body of Christ different in history and tradition from the recent centuries of the evangelical movement. An understanding of the full gospel comes only out of life together in the fullness of the body of Christ. Partial perspectives—"heresies" as they are tradition-ally called—are the natural fruit of detached body parts that de-clare "I have no need of you." Evangelicals need ecumenicals for the mutual sharing of charisms, ecclesial and doctrinal.

And vice versa. So we move to the admonitions evangelicals have to bring to ecumenicals.[27]

Evangelical Admonitions

It is better for a card-carrying evangelical to give these admon-ishments to ecumenicals, but as an evangelical ecumenical I shall do my best to state the counterpoint needed in matters of mutual correction, albeit in shorter compass than the forego-ing, as my primary charge is to bring an ecumenical perspective on evangelicalism. The admonitions have a kind of parallel to the foregoing. I begin with worldly temptation of ecumenicals, then proceed to some seductions to which ecumenicals regu-larly succumb related to the very admonitions they (we) are ready to give to evangelicals.

Worldly Ecumenicals

Ecumenicals come by their worldliness explicitly, in contrast to evangelicals for whom it works its ways implicitly. It is built into an ecumenical hermeneutic and history. That is, ec-umenism as a twentieth-century movement given impetus by old-line traditions and denominations always had culture/soci-ety/contemporaneity in its sights. Using the World Council of Churches as a marker, the 1948 assembly took as its title, "Man's Disorder and God's Design."[28] The same larger stream of ecumenism had its "Life and Work" as well as its "Faith and Order" agenda and institutions. Put theologically, the "world" as well as Scripture and tradition was/is an element in its authority structure. Of course, each of the elements—Bible, church, world[29]—has a different status and role: In ecumenical theology the Bible is declared to be the *source* of authority, the church and its traditions the *resource*, and the world the *setting*.[30] The function of the "world" is catalysis, providing the context and questions in which the church out of its Scripture listens for and speaks a timely Word. *However!*

This "however" is the reminder evangelicals bring to ecumenicals. Has the biblical Word been regularly and faithfully spoken by the church, ecumenical and old-line? The record does not bear it out. As noted, the Barmen Declaration of 1934 has been looked to by historic ecumenism as the model for its witness. Yet the principal author of that confession that challenged the blood-and-soil philosophy that was making inroads into the churches in Germany, Karl Barth, gave a stirring speech at the Amsterdam assembly warning that the *world* was setting the ecumenical agenda rather than the *one Word*. Reinhold Niebuhr, in turn, spoke passionately in defense of the importance of a cultural agenda for a faithful church with a biblical faith. And so the tension has continued within ecumenism. In my view both were right, Niebuhr arguing for the contextuality of the gospel, but Barth warning that the tail too often wags the dog.

Barth's concerns should have been taken more seriously than they were. Agencies and assemblies of the World Council of Churches have from time to time been tempted to let the world both set the agenda and call the meeting, a cultural accommodation that weakened its ties to its Orthodox members, and has had its impact on its general support and funding. The temptation has afflicted not only global ecumenism, but other wings of conciliar Christianity, national, regional, and local, and its partner old-line denominational bureaucracies. The problem is the temptation to reverse the Word and world, with the *Zeitgeist* taken as source and norm.

Mesmerism with the Now, the context, the New, and the consequent diminishment of the classical touchstones of Christian faith—Scripture and tradition and their witness to Jesus Christ—is evident in the following representative areas. We noted the counsels ecumenicals have for evangelicals regarding their exclusivity and us-and-them mentality. However, ecumenicals regularly succumb to their counterparts' theological indifferentism and the blurring of critical lines that must be drawn in the sand. Again, I speak from the inside of ecumenical/mainline struggles that need a clear and bold evangelical word.

Social Reductionism

I begin with the social species of the genus "worldly ecumenical." The admonition has to do with the temptation that goes with the ecumenical critique of convertive piety. That is, the ecumenical/old-line preoccupation with social context, the focus on the systemic ethical issues, easily slides into a neglect of the personal dimension of Christian faith and witness. And more, it invites the kind of adaptation to current social currents earlier described, the succumbing to powerful cultural ideologies.

The evolution of the concept of *mission* in the 1960s in ecumenical circles is a vivid illustration of how the "social" came to exclude the personal. As a participant in the World Council of Churches' "Missionary Structure of the Congregation" study, I watched *mission* come to mean participation in the social struggles of the hour to the exclusion of the call to conversion and the evangelism imperative.[31] This horizontalizing of mission came to include on the part of the self-described ecclesial "revolutionaries" (in contrast to the "reformers" and "renewers") the replacing of the local congregation (only involved, they said, in the irrelevancies of "hatching, matching, and dispatching"—baptism, marriage, and burial) by "new forms" of mission geared to the battles for "being, having, and belonging"—war, poverty, and race. Much of my own writing and involvement in mission in the '60s and '70s was an effort to redress this exclusion and imbalance with a holistic "Word and deed" missiology in colleagueship with evangelicals like Orlanda Costas.[32]

Inclusivity and Ideology

Paul's Letter to the Galatians teaches that "there is no longer male and female; for you are all one in Christ" (3:28). That message is getting through in church life today. A particular challenge associated with it is learning to welcome the charism that women bring to the body of Christ today without accession to an ideological feminism that demands that all Christian doctrine must be redone in fealty to its norm.

"Inclusive language" is a laboratory of learning about where the line must be drawn between relating to, and capitulating to, the call to gender inclusivity. For example, the ecumenical movement has produced a New Revised Standard Version of the Bible which seeks to retain authorial intention throughout, as in the retention of the language of Father and Son, but reads "men" passages with the same standard, framed in Galatians 3 terms, as "men and women." Yet others believe that gender inclusivity requires much more, ranging from adding "Mother" to "Father" in biblical texts, in creeds, in the revision of old hymns and in new hymns, or yet further excising all "Father" and "Son" language in Scripture, in the baptismal formula, in confessions, in hymns, and in substituting presumed inclusive language such as "Creator, Redeemer, and Sanctifier" for the Trinity and the baptismal formula (in fact, Arian in doctrine), or maternal language and imagery for God, or even further, judging the word *God* itself as patriarchal and either balancing it with "Goddess" or substituting the latter for the former.[33]

Behind these distortions lies the penetration of contemporary ideology into mainline/ecumenical circles, now organized in such fora as the Re-imagining conferences (to be sharply distinguished from the fresh corporate effort by women of faith as in the gender-reconciliation project led by Mary Stewart Van Leeuwen).[34] When "women's experience" as defined by such becomes normative for the church and the faith, we have a moment when Barmen's word must again be spoken: Jesus Christ is the *one* Word we have to trust and obey in life and death. Evangelicals, often in partnership with evangelical ecumenicals, have spoken that admonitory word in the current christological movements in ecumenical and old-line settings, as in the "Confessing Christ" movement in my own denomination.[35] And they must speak it ever and again. Counsel us, with

Karl Barth's help, that biblical language is not the lengthened shadow of human experience, masculine or feminine, but has an integrity of its own to be interpreted as Scripture uses such language according to the norm of Jesus Christ. Help the ecumenical/old-line churches to draw a clear line between Galatians-like christological construals and obeisance to current ideological trends.[36]

Pluralism and the Scandal of Particularity

The religious response to the crisis through which our country is now passing is a showcase of the need for evangelical witness. We can thank God for the outpouring of both prayer and care from ecumenical/mainline as well as evangelical churches and leaders, as well as the cry of protest and concern from Jewish, Muslim, and other religious traditions. But I register my concern here about too much of the theology at work in my own old-line church reaction, in its well-intentioned efforts to show solidarity with those of other religious beliefs, and specifically the needed sympathy with Muslims being tarred with the atrocities of a fanatical few. "Ecumenical" efforts too often seemed to erase any meaningful distinction among the religions, morphing into doctrinal indifferentism. For example, in three passionate and well-intentioned religious messages to constituents from one regional leader of my denomination, no mention of "Christ" was made. And that from my church named "The United Church of Christ"? We need to hear, amidst the necessary caring, compassion, and challenge to religious hate, an evangelical warning about dissolving the saving singularity of Jesus Christ. We cannot abandon John 14:6, the "scandal of particularity" as it has been called, Christ as the definitive way, truth, and life. Ironically, the eliminating of particularistic claims that purports to be Christian charity toward other religions is, actually, a covert dismissal of the truth claims of other religions as well as the Christian faith. Eliminating such claims denies any claim to particularity, swallowed up as such by the Enlightenment ideology of a common core to all faiths, the differences being trivial, or worse, the postmodern assumption that no religious truth is accessible, each community or person doing "what works for them," or "works for me." From evangelicals we need a clear admonition to steward Christian claims to truth in the midst of our works of love for the religious neighbor in need, to "speak the truth in love."

And again, a needed evangelical admonition that this crisis underscores has to do with the flip side of the tolerance for ambiguity for which ecumenical/mainline theology is known. The stress on the faults common to all sides in a dispute, and the need for self-criticism, can also eventuate in the incapacity to act decisively and to challenge evil unambiguously. Thus the trumpet may give an uncertain sound just when a call to "resist the powers of evil" is required, as in the present conflict with the forces of terrorism. Spokespersons for mainline churches, often reflecting a reenergized anti-globalization movement now turning uncritically pacifist, fall in step with pleas for a peaceful solution, ultimately correct, but penultimately naive in the extreme. Evangelicals need to admonish such ecumenicals that ambiguity cannot cloud the need for an either-or decision in the face of the slaughter of innocents in this war against terrorism.

Conclusion

As I ruminated about all the foregoing, I began to wonder if there is anything like this conference in self-defined ecumenical circles. Are evangelicals invited to come to ecumenicals with their admonitions? For example, do ecumenicals ask, as is asked here, what might be learned from fundamentalists?[37] The mutuality that is sought by ecumenicals in the interaction of diverse denominations does not have much, if any, counterpart in ecumenical initiative toward evangelicals.[38] Surely there is an irony here, and a role reversal. Evangelicals, seeking out "pilgrims on the sawdust trail," can teach ecumenicals about ecumenism and the mutuality of affirmation and admonition. Thank you for your charism. May we continue to journey on that sawdust trail together.

11

Can Anything Good Come Out of Liberalism?

One Pilgrim's Regress

Thomas C. Oden

We are all here seeking to clarify the unity of the body of Christ in a fuller way than has been accessible in the era in which our various streams of church memory have remained inattentive to each other. The premise of the conference from which this volume grew was: If we all speak the truth in love out of these various streams, we may reach a fuller understanding of Christian identity than if we settled for thinking separately within our separated communions.

We have indeed been long separated by historical, ecclesiological, and sociological differences, but the Spirit is inviting us to a new form of conversation, to new depths of listening to each other, and to hearing the groaning of the Spirit for us, and speaking to each other without any sacrifice of conscience or intellect.

Whatever Became of Liberalism?

What can evangelicals and pentecostals and Catholics and the faithful of the mainline learn from each other? Then I am asked, and here is the curve ball: what good can come from liberalism? To me of all people. I have not since the early seventies been asked to speak a good word for liberalism or situation ethics or demythology. We are trying to bring into conversation six sectors of Christian understanding: evangelicals, Reformed, fundamentalists, pentecostals, mainline Protestant, and Catholics. But liberals? We are too soon tempted to give up.

I accepted the title I was given without fully considering its ramifications. As one who every day is writing and arguing for a tough critique of the failures of the liberal tradition, it is ironic that I would be given the humbling job of asking whether anything good can come out of liberalism. My rhetorical energies have for a quarter of a century been poured into combating the theological myopias of liberalism. That is where I am on familiar ground, and would prefer to be.

In my more generous moments I think I can still say some good things that can come out of liberalism, but it is not easy for me—it is a forced effort. So I take this as a penitential exercise.

I affirm the good intentions of liberalism on fairness, democracy, and inclusion, though I am well aware of how this intent has often fallen short of full actualization.

When I speak of liberalism I am recalling the liberal church within which I have been baptized, nurtured, and educated. I am speaking out of my own mainline Protestant tradition, arguably one of the more liberal of the churches of the mainline, of those that still prop up the National Council of Churches and World Council of Churches with large injections of emergency funding. If you were to read the literature of the official agencies of the United Methodist Church, especially the Women's Division of the General Board of Global Ministry and the Board of Church and Society, you would still find a strident liberalism that I view as a deterioration of liberalism at its best. I do not want to allow liberalism to be represented rhetorically by its most radical voices. If you just read that literature, you would conclude that liberalism is saturated with Marxist metaphors and methods, a bold polemic against capitalism and market economics, a romantic vision of socialist and statist economies, and an almost absolute conformity to the platform of the Democratic Party and more so to the left wing of that party. United Methodist leadership might generously be said to be the Democratic Party at prayer, but that assumes that someone is praying, which at times seems a stretch. It is more like the Democratic Party caught in a moment of moral self-justification. It is these excesses that have in fact gone sour, and that have required renewal and confessing movements in every mainline church.

But are these voices an adequate expression of liberalism? I think not. I was baptized into the one holy catholic apostolic church that spoke in generous accents of the fatherhood of God and the brotherhood of man. My baptism in the name of the Father, Son, and Holy Spirit was not regarded as defective by Catholics but it was by Baptists. The hymnody and liturgy I learned was entirely orthodox, as it was derived principally from the Anglican liturgy, magnified by the great hymns of the Wesleyan revivalism. The liturgies of the liberal church still contain substantive reference to the incarnation, the atonement, ascension, and return of the Lord for final judgment, even when left-wing theologians ignore these. In my denomination we have a particular constitutional guarantee that says that the general legislative body cannot amend our doctrinal standards, which are clearly defined as "The Twenty-five Articles of Religion," *Wesley's Standard Sermons, Explanatory Notes Upon the New Testament,* and the "General Rules of the Methodist Societies." These are fixed texts that no legislation can amend, and to which every ordained minister is solemnly pledged to know and defend, and to which every United Methodist bishop is honor bound to guard and guarantee. Of course, they do not. That is the problem.[1]

Oddly, the great strength of the liberal tradition into which I was baptized was the strength of cohesive church discipline. It is this cohesion that the extreme left is now disavowing. This is why I am a founding participant in the Confessing movement within the United Methodist Church, which has this purpose: "Confessing Jesus Christ as Son, Savior, and Lord, the Confessing Movement exists to enable the United Methodist Church to retrieve its classical doctrinal identity, and to live it out as disciples of Jesus Christ."

Those who best typify liberalism are William Elery Channing, Ralph Waldo Emerson, Alfred Loisy, D. F. Strauss, Fritz

Buri, Paul Tillich, Rudolf Bultmann, Karl Holl, Albert Schweitzer, Martin Kahler, Samuel Taylor Coleridge, Ernst Troeltsch, Adolf von Harnack, and H. R. MacIntosh. I gasp. I plead for time. Liberalism's key linking terms are enlightenment, idealism, naturalism, and utilitarianism. The tradition goes back to Grotius, Schleiermacher, and who knows else—even Adam Smith. The apex year of liberalism was 1848 in the German tradition! That is the time of Horace Bushnell's writing of *Christian Nurture* in 1847 and *God in Christ* in 1849, where Bushnell borrowed from Schleiermacher's view of the Trinity and from Emerson's romanticism to become the father of American theological liberalism of the nineteenth century. Many achievements have come out of that tradition, although it has yielded its share of bitter fruit and disappointments.

Though freedom is the hallmark of liberal rhetoric, it is ironic that liberals have given so much effort to control of economic processes by political means. Hence there has been an increasing tendency of the recent liberal tradition to be drawn to socialist thought and statist-controlled economies.

The fixed idea of change is central to liberalism. It can be democratic change or revolutionary change, but liberalism is always focused on change. This puts the liberal already and always in some sort of tension with any classical view, hence any sacred text, or any attempt to guard a depositum of faith or to retrieve an apostolic tradition.

Liberals want to utilize government as an instrument of economic redistribution and social change, whether by executive, legislative, or judicial control. Liberalism wants to plan and guide change, often unaware of the temptations of the planners to plan their own interests into the plans. Liberals are all too willing to experiment, both with their own lives, their children's, and with everyone else's. While liberal rhetoric seems to fight authority, they constantly work to expand state authority. They fight dogma but cling to their own dogmas of toleration and egalitarian idealism. Alfred North Whitehead wrote of liberal theology that it "confined itself to the suggestion of vapid reasons why people should go to church in the traditional way."[2] Richard Niebuhr's statement, "A God without wrath brought men without sin into the kingdom without judgment through the ministrations of a Christ without a cross,"[3] is still one of the best descriptions of liberalism. After tracking the theological tradition from Harnack to Barth, Walter Marshall Horton wrote in 1934:

> It is ungrateful to speak disparagingly about this type of religious thought, for we still talk and think, in the very act of condemning it, in words and phrases borrowed from the liberal dictionary. . . . Yet it is very plain already that they are dead concepts. . . . They have not died as a result of any concerted, effective attack upon their validity, but simply as the result of a general change in the intellectual climate. . . . Their truth and their value will outlive them, . . . but it must now be announced, as an accomplished fact, regrettable but duly certified, that their vital sap has departed from them.[4]

He ends his essay "The Decline of Liberalism" with a letter from a liberal denominational executive who was noticing among his colleagues "a feeling of theological homelessness."

> The note of earnestness and conviction, not to say enthusiasm, is missing in pulpit utterances. For instance, one of the . . . men called me aside after one of the seminars and said that for the last two years he had repeatedly been impelled to call his people together after church and say to them that they were at liberty to get any good out of what he had been saying that they found it possible to receive, but that in honesty he wanted to tell them that he didn't believe it himself.

Many liberals are looking for orthodox roots. Many are dispirited. They await a welcoming hand from us. They, too, long for a deeper participation in Christ. Some liberal Catholics are willing to be instructed by traditional Catholic moral teaching. Some liberal Protestants are frightened by liberal excesses, and want to return to the center.

I want to make a bridge between the liberal past and the orthodox-Catholic-evangelical future, and to determine what that portends for the new ecumenism. I am under deep conviction that we stand in a unique moment of opportunity, in the light of what is happening in the extraordinary new situation of ecumenical self-definition following the withdrawal of Bob Edgar's name from the Marriage Initiative, after the National Council of Churches' unresolved financial crisis, and after meetings of the World Council of Churches in Harare, Zimbabwe. We are all being called to as yet unsounded depths of ecumenical reflection. Gabriel Fackre has discussed an ecumenical view of evangelicals. I now speak from the vantage point of an evangelical within the mainline.

The Return of a Once-Liberated Pilgrim

I have used for this essay the subtitle of "One Pilgrim's Regress." The phrase invites me to reflect on my own personal history of return, not to my past but to the future promises of the historic past. It is more a reflection on growth in grace than regress. It is only regress if you consider liberalism progress. I have indeed regressed from liberal fantasies. But if you consider liberalism a deterioration of classic Christianity, then it is progress to transcend it, but that is not progress in the usual liberal definition, which relies largely upon human ingenuity to solve social problems, and expects the trend toward command economies to continue into the indefinite future and influence all future societies.

My assignment is to provide a personal narrative of my metanoia and of my turning toward the faith of orthodoxy with lowercase. It offers opportunity to hold up before God our thanks that so many lives are being changed by the gospel.[5] I offer my story as modest evidence of one life whose liberal direction has been radically reversed by the unexpected discovery of classic ecumenical teaching. My own personal story has become intertwined with and dependent upon classic consensual exegesis. That is what I want to explain.

Liberal Roots, Revolutionary Mentors

I grew up in far southwestern Oklahoma, only twelve miles from the Texas border, where the hills roll gently, the purple Quartz Mountains rise in the distance, the fields are green with wheat in February and white with cotton in September, and an older rural culture is still intact, a culture that has been lost in the urban maze. In the 1930s this was a place where doors were often left unlocked, and where the neighbor's word was his bond.

Since my parents were incredibly caring and godly, I avoided the adolescent pitfall of absurdly rebelling against them. But they themselves were highly independent mavericks, pious, quiet radicals. My father was a populist when Oklahoma was tending toward rural populist socialism in the tradition of the Wisconsin farmer-labor party (quite different from the social-radical politics of Huey Long). This evolutionary socialism, more in the tradition of Norman Thomas and Henry Wallace than of Marx or Lenin, gave him a deep distrust of concentrations of wealth. My mother, of blessed memory, taught piano to hundreds of Anglos, blacks, and Hispanics in our small town.

For me Marxism became radicalized early in the 1950s, during the time of Ho Chi Minh, whom I idolized as an agrarian communist patriot more than ten years before the American entry into the Vietnam War. Long before Vietnam I was a very active pacifist, outraged by Hiroshima, organizing pacifist groups along the lines of the Fellowship of Reconciliation.[6] In those days I got my agnosticism from Nietzsche and Robert Ingersoll, and my social idealism from radical Methodists.[7]

As one who was presumably teaching Christian theology and ethics in the early sixties, my heart was focused upon social change, and the politicizing of the mission of the church. While I was supposedly being paid to be a Christian theologian, my social vision was basically Marxist, my psychology was Freudian, my understanding of the change process was mostly Rogerian, and my ethic was situationist-Nietzschean. I was a thoroughly and narrowly modern. I was only pretending to be a theologian. I was in love with heresy.

My motivation for entering the ministry was nine-tenths political. I saw the church as a potential instrument of social change. My interest in theology was primarily in whatever ways I could see to take it and its institutions captive to liberal political ideals. I was one of those little men with big ideas, with hardly the vaguest notion of how they might be implemented.

After Yale, while something deep in my heart remained intuitively Barthian, my head was spinning with Heidegger. My scriptural knowledge came from Bultmann, my social vision from Tillich, and when I confessed my sins it was in a Niebuhrian voice. I was neo-orthodox to the core, but not orthodox.

I recall in 1962 at an ecumenical InterSeminary Conference at the Southwestern Baptist Theological Seminary, when Dr. Robert Naylor was president, I was asked to speak in chapel before their vast audience of two thousand students. I was then deep into a romantic view of secularization, Bonhoeffer, and the end of religion. These were theological temptations I took a long time outgrowing. I preached on a Johannine text on worldly Christianity, and on "letting the world set the agenda." After I finished, Dr. Naylor, in his warm, congenial, and pastoral way, got up and deftly refuted practically every point I had made. Now that I look back on it I can see that virtually all the points he made were right on target, and he was well advised to warn his students against my bland thoughts about universal salvation, humanistic optimism, and simplistic situation ethics.

Comparative Trajectories of Two Methodist Radicals

It was not until I recently explained to some twenty-something students how closely my path followed the same trajectory as that of Hillary Rodham Clinton that they grasped what I was saying about my political history. It seems odd now, but she was working out of precisely the same sources and moving in the same circles as I was in our earlier years. I predated her by several years, but our two trajectories are almost a mirror image up until the early seventies. I fell harder for Marxist ideology than she did, but we had many of the same stops along the way: Tillich's cultural analysis, Bultmann's demythology, early feminism, and, of course, a lot of secularization theology. By simple comparison with the highly public views of Hillary Rodham Clinton, it is easy to see where I once was located ideologically, only later to reverse and disavow this location. My education was remarkably parallel to hers (Yale, Methodist activism, moving ever leftward politically), both in the ideas we jointly held and the key people by whom we were mentored.

We were both avid followers of Saul Alinsky, the pragmatic urban organizer and unprincipled amoralist. Hillary became intrigued by situation ethics, the subject on which I wrote my Yale dissertation. She learned her tough amoral activism from Alinsky and her view of history from quasi-Marxists, just as I did. She once revealed that she had saved every copy of *Motive* magazine, the progenitor of much of her religious and political radicalism, and so have I, editors Roger Ortmayer and B. J. Styles being old friends of mine. *Motive* fueled me intellectually during my heady years as a pacifist, existentialist, Tillichian, and proto-Marxist. I trusted the Methodist radicalism of motive. It set the leftist momentum and pace of all my thinking, as it did for Clinton.

Senator Clinton's chief mentors in Chicago included dear friends of mine, Joe and Lynn Mathews, and their associates in the Ecumenical Institute of Austin, Texas, later the Ecumenical Institute of Chicago, where some of my writings were embedded in the standard curriculum. When I look now at Clinton's persistent ethical contextualism, messianism, statist social idealism, and her pragmatic toughness, I see a mirror of myself a few decades ago.[8]

An Unexpected Journey

In the early 1970s I went through what seemed to me a lonely, almost solitary, pilgrimage—lonely for me because I was the only one I knew who was going through it. This radical reversal moved me from obsessive spiritual faddism to stable classic Christian teaching. After a long period of turning, it finally brought me back to classic Christianity, and resulted in the publication of *Agenda for Theology, Pastoral Theology,* four volumes of *Classical Pastoral Care,* and the three volumes of *Systematic Theology.*

As a movement theologian, I had joined one movement after another, whether political, therapeutic, or philosophical. I assumed that some vast social revolution was impending. I thought some radical change was required, necessary, and inevitable. As a former convinced proponent of the radical demythologizing biblical criticism of Rudolf Bultmann (on whose work I wrote my doctoral dissertation), I am now trying to repent of the bad habit of reading Scripture through modern eyes. For years I tried to read the New Testament without the premises of incarnation and resurrection (that's very hard to do).

Before and after Doctrinal Contrition

My intention now is to revisit that earlier liberal period in my personal story before I became immersed in the study of the ecumenical councils and ancient consensual exegesis. The fantasy was the assumption that some vast social revolution was impending. I thought radical change was required, necessary, and inevitable. Like John Spong later, I thought Christianity must change or die. I thought my task as a theologian was to undermine conservative institutional structures and lead the way to their imagined reconstruction along humanistic lines. I will contrast the concerns I had then with the vocation I have undertaken since the ancient Christian writers became serious partners in dialogue for me.

It is amusing now to contrast the concerns I had then with the vocation I have undertaken since the ancient Christian writers became my constant companions. If now I slightly exaggerate differences between the before and after, my intent is to offer an accurate description of my decisive reversal, without allowing it to die the death of a thousand qualifications. I do not disavow the providence of God working within my former Freudian, Marxist, existentialist, and demythologizing past, or fail to see grace leading me through and beyond it. Rather I celebrate that liberal history as having been taken up into a more inclusive understanding of history and divine-human encounter.

Did I say "inclusive"? That word remains the key shibboleth of my liberated colleagues. They sought to be inclusive but did so only within the strict limits of modern ideologies trapped in reductive naturalism. In this captivity they systematically excluded pre-modern wisdoms, assumptions, and values. In contrast, I experience a gracious sense of multigenerational inclusion in the communion of saints that antecedes and transcends modern life and that will survive its death. The faithful belong to a much more inclusive communion than is even conceivable within the limits of modern ideologies.

What Happened between Then and Now

Then I distrusted even the faint smell of orthodoxy. I was in love with heresy, the wilder, the more seductive.

Now I have come to trust the consensus I once distrusted. It is a reliable consensus of scriptural interpreters, double-checked and reconfirmed over many generations. I now relish studying the diverse rainbow of orthodox voices from varied cultures spanning all continents, all epochs over two thousand years. I happily embrace the term *orthodoxy*. This has become for me a refreshing experience of liberation to classic Christianity after a long imprisonment in the more closed worldview of modern limits. This is not a minor reversal.

I used to think my modern methods and values gained from my Yale and Heidelberg education to be quite an obvious improvement over all those archaic views of the first millennium. I had stereotyped all of the ancient Christian exegetes with spurious charges of extreme allegorization that applied to only a few of them. I now thrive constantly on their letters, homilies, prayers, songs, commentaries, and moral reasoning.

Earlier I had learned to be defensive in relation to the two most basic premises of the New Testament: the incarnate Word and the risen Lord. Now I esteem nothing higher than the written word as ecumenically received and consensually explicated. Now when I teach my brightest Ph.D. students, I have nothing better to offer than the written word as viewed through the unfolding meeting of brilliant and classic minds freely consenting in varied cultures and times to that apostolic testimony—the minds of the likes of Irenaeus, Athanasius, and Ambrose.

Once I thought of pastoral preaching as reasoning existentially about humanistic personal and social change. Now I see that the best pastoral preaching is focused on testimony canonically received and grasped by the believing community of all times and places. That seed will bear fruit in its own time. That word will address these hearers directly in its own distinctive way as long as it is not accompanied by too much static from me.

Mere Christianity understands itself to be both pre-Freudian and post-Freudian, pre-Marxist and post-Marxist, both pre-fundamentalist and post-fundamentalist. It is post-neo-anything since the further one "progresses" from ancient apostolic testimony, the more hopeless becomes the human condition.

The Turnaround

The pivot occurred when my irascible, endearing Jewish mentor, my colleague at Drew, Will Herberg, straightforwardly told me what Protestant colleagues must have been too polite to say, that I would remain densely uneducated until I had studied carefully Athanasius, Ambrose, Basil, and Cyril of Alexandria. With his usual gruff voice he repeatedly said something like this: "Tom, you have not yet met the great minds of your own tradition. Just as I, after my communist days, found it important to carefully read Talmud and the Midrashim to discover who I was as a Jew, you will have to sit down with the ancient Christian writers to discover who you are as a believer. Without this solid textual grounding, you will become lost in supposed relevance. If you are going to deepen to become a working theologian instead of a know-it-all contemporary pundit, you had best get at it, and until you do, you are not a theologian except in name, even if remunerated as one."

That was in the early seventies, when with long hair, bobbles, bangles, and beads, and a gleam of communitarian utopianism in my eyes, I came upon the fourth-century treatise by Nemesius, *Peri phuseos anthropon* (On the Nature of the Human), when it at length dawned on me that ancient psychological wisdom could be the basis for a deeper critique of modern narcissistic psychological individualism than I had yet seen.

If you had asked me then what my life might look like now, I would have guessed dead wrong. Grace and providence hedged life far more toward unpredictable outcomes than I had ever then imagined. At that time I never dreamed that I would someday learn to grant to Scripture its own distinctive premises: divine sovereignty, revelation, incarnation, resurrection, and final judgment.

I had been taught that these premises were precisely what had to be transcended, circumvented, and danced around in order to communicate with the modern mind. I had learned to dance the strange oscillation of Tillich and Bultmann. I was taught by example that the Scripture interpreter exists to protect the modern hearer from the text, and to provide some alternative explanation of the text fitting within modern assumptions. Now I revel in the very premises I once had carefully learned to set aside and bury and rationalize away: the preexistent Logos, the triune mystery, the radical depth of sin passing through the generations, the risen Lord, the grace of baptism. As I worked my way through these beautiful, long-hidden texts of classic Christianity, the deeper, perennial questions resurfaced. I reemerged out of the secularizing maze to once again delight in the holy mysteries of the faith, and in the recurrent puzzles of human existence. Rather than interpreting the texts, the texts began to interpret me.[9] I was amazed. With Charles Wesley, I asked:

> And can it be that I could gain
> An interest in the Savior's blood,
> Died he for me, who caused him pain,
> For me who him to death pursued?
> Amazing love, how can it be,
> That thou my God shouldst die for me?

Long after receiving my Ph.D. in theology at Yale under Richard Niebuhr's direction, long after I had for years pretended to be a theologian, after I had published books on theology, and had been teaching theology for more than ten years—something happened. What was it—a reversal; a conversion; a repentance? Whatever it might be called, it occurred only incrementally, like a mustard seed growing.

An Enlarged Freedom of Inquiry

What shifted? Psychologically the shift moved from Freudian, Rogerian, and Skinnerian values, especially individualistic self-actualization and narcissistic self-expression, toward engendering durable habits of moral excellence in an actual covenant community. Methodologically I shifted away from individualist culture-bound experience and toward the publicly shared texts of Scripture and ecumenical tradition. In justice issues I moved decisively away from trust in regulatory power and rationalistic planning and more toward reasoning out of the concrete histories of suffering persons, many of whom had been damaged by my own idealism. All these shifts had intuitively happened by about 1972–73, but I had much more yet to learn.

I now experience greater, not less, cross-cultural freedom of inquiry, because I stand within the blessed presence of the communion of saints of all generations. I am now emancipated to investigate subjects previously blocked from investigation within narrow modern biases: God's foreknowledge, revelation in history, demonic temptation, the lives of saints, and angelic succor. These have become my daily bread.

I am now steeped in inquiry into the vast chorus of rabbinic and classical Christian interpretations of the sacred text. I now swim in the creative orthodoxy mediated through brilliant voices of other times and places. I celebrate a refreshing liberation to orthodoxy and freedom from narrow modern dogmatisms. I have glimpsed the gracious flexibility of the centered teaching of the classic exegetes. Again and again they appear to be Spirit-led to an amazing equilibrium in their attentiveness to the whole course of sacred Scripture. This orthodox matrix now melds into all that I do. It finds itself at home in every conceivable cultural and intellectual environment, without ceasing to offer anew the unchanging eternal word in each new historical setting.

What changed? A simple, 180-degree reversal in attentiveness to the text of Scripture in a way that would challenge my modern narrowness. Before the mid-seventies I had been steadily asking questions on the hidden premise of four key value assumptions of modern consciousness: hedonic self-actualization, autonomous individualism, reductive naturalism, and absolute moral relativism. Now my questions about decaying modern culture are being decisively shaped by the counterpremises of the most trusted ancient consensual scriptural interpreters of classic Christianity: redemptive sacrifice; knowing through a worshiping community; theocentric reordering of values; refusing idolatries; listening for catholic consensus.

The Old Ecumenism Made New

In those days, I used to think of myself as a bona fide ecumenist, having grown up in the ecumenical movement of the days of W. A. Visser, Henry Pitt Van Dusen, G. Bromley Oxnam, William C. Martin, Charles West, and Paul Albrecht. These were my ecumenical mentors. I was an avid interseminary participant in the Evanston WCC General Assembly of 1954, and in the Geneva World Conference on Church and Society of 1966, and in various consultations at the Ecumenical Institute at Bossey, Switzerland. It took me a long time to learn, however, that I was at that time committed merely to the twentieth-century ecumenical movement with its extremely accommodative mentality toward modern ideologies, and with its tragic aversion to ancient ecumenism.

I now am reluctantly convinced that my youthful form of bureaucratic ecumenism was anti-ecumenical, viewed from the standpoint of the ancient ecumenical tradition. I am not demonizing these forsaken ideologies so much as recognizing the demonic in my own history, my own self. I have followed the curious steps of my once-Communist then later rabinically grounded conservative Jewish mentor Will Herberg. I am recognizing a fair amount of self-delusion and demonic deception in ideologies that once appeared seductive.

In the last three decades I have often felt like a lonely and secluded bridge builder between vast continents of separated religious traditions, and like a translator between remote dialects, conflicting historical vocabularies, moral languages, and ecclesial mind-sets. But many have joined me on what once seemed a lonely journey.

Ironically it was the liberal-activist heritage that gave me my triune baptismal faith and my first Christian vocabulary. This memory remains highly valued, even if transcended. However far I may have departed from it (in its pacifist, existentialist, psychoanalytic, and quasi-Marxist expressions), I will always be its grateful son.

The Councils Showed the Way

It was from reading the texts of the canons of the ecumenical councils that I first intuitively grasped the social dynamics of orthodoxy later to be spelled out by Vincent. It was in 1972 that I first read through the fourteen volumes of the *Nicene and Post-Nicene Fathers*. It is an unadorned report of the canons of the ecumenical councils and significant regional councils that fed into the great general councils of the first millennium. I read it straight through in a few days of engrossed concentration, and have never been the same person since.

Those were among the most important days of my life. That reading effected literally everything else I would touch as a teacher, writer, and editor for the rest of my life. For there it first dawned upon me how conciliar boundaries were marked, and how ecumenical decisions were rendered. The canons themselves did not detail the process that led up to them. But there remain many clues embedded in these texts that reveal the main assumptions and motifs of this process. It was about this time that I found my way back to the *Commonitory* of Vincent of Lérins. Only then did I see explicated for the first time in a clear and systematic way the ecumenical way of truth that I knew to be already operative in the Ecumenical Councils.

Ever since then I have remained committed to unoriginality. This is an imperative that appears in every book I have written since the mid-seventies: a commitment not to offer anything original. That is not a joke but a solemn pledge. I am trying to learn to make no pretense of "improving" upon the apostles.

The Abiding Conversation

It seems dull now to confess that this radical reversal took place through quiet reading in early mornings, and in long conversations with the faithful (mostly my Orthodox, Catholic, and evangelical students). Several moments reckon high among the glimmer of new birth: While reading John of Damascus on the *oikonomia* of God (in *The Orthodox Faith*), I belatedly realized that the reordering of theological ideas I fondly imagined I was just then inventing had been well understood as a received tradition in the eighth century. While reading John Chrysostom on voluntary poverty I discovered that Peter Berger's sociological theory of knowledge had long ago been intuited and accurately described. While reading Cyril of Jerusalem's *Catechetical Lecture* on evidences for the resurrection, I became persuaded that Pannenberg had provided a more accurate account than Bultmann of the event of resurrection. While reading fourth-century Sister Macrina, and of the women surrounding Jerome, I traced the profound influences of women on the earliest and richest traditions of spiritual formation, especially in monastic and ascetic disciplines. While reading Augustine's *City of God* on the ironic providences of history I finally grasped how right was Solzhenitsyn on the spiritual promise of Russia.

And so it went. Every question that I thought was new and unprecedented I found had already been much investigated, and had left a profound textual residue. The result was alive in the intergenerational wisdom of the ancient community of faith, which I learned still persists as a living community of interpretation.

Earlier I had focused intently as a theologian upon psychological analysis. I had put so much trust in these methods (psychoanalysis, behaviorism, and client-centered therapy). At long last I came to behold interpersonal transactions and personal dynamics in the light of God's becoming fully human in the incarnation, becoming the theandric (divine-human) One in whom human personhood is most fully actualized and understood. This incarnational revolution suddenly invaded every corner of my psychological research.

Once blown by every wind of doctrine and preoccupied with therapeutic fads and the spirit of hypertoleration, I came by grace to grasp the distinctive way of patient consensual reasoning that occurs normatively within classic Christianity. I became fascinated with the social dynamics of orthodoxy, the transmission of apostolic tradition, and the received canons of classic consensual religious teaching.

When the Lord tore the kingdom of Israel from Saul, Samuel declared: "He who is the Glory of Israel does not lie or change his mind; for he is not a man, that he should change his mind" (1 Sam. 15:29). God's constant, attentive, holy love is eternally unchanging. Slowly awakening to the bright immutability of God's responsive covenant love is precisely what has changed for me. Yahweh must have laughed in addressing the heirs of the old rascal Jacob with this ironic word: "I the Lord do not change. So you, O descendants of Jacob, are not destroyed" (Mal. 3:6). If God's purposes were constantly revisable, how could the faithful rely upon them? Still it is so: "Every good and perfect gift is from above, coming down from the Father of the heavenly lights, who does not change like shifting shadows" (James 1:17). What has changed in my personal history is recognition of the unchanging character of God.

Part 6

EVANGELICALS
IN THE MAINLINE

12

Up the Creek

Paddling in the Maelstrom of the Mainline

Paul F. M. Zahl

The fate of evangelical Christians within mainline Christian churches has seldom been a happy one. The Church of England pulled it off, in an almost unique instance, with the appointment of evangelical diocesan bishops in the mid–nineteenth century. The established (Lutheran) church of Wüntemberg in Germany was also able to accommodate evangelicals or "pietists" in its mainstream from the seventeenth century. There are one or two other cases on record. But no more. Usually, the bloodstream of the mainline contains antibodies that reject evangelicals.

This short essay speaks to the current condition of evangelicals within the American mainline churches. The prognosis is extremely serious, possibly terminal. Yet the author has to maintain that there is always hope.

As an Episcopalian cathedral dean, my field of vision is (P)ECUSA, or the (Protestant) Episcopal Church in the U.S.A.[1] But my friends in the United Methodist Church and in the Presbyterian Church in the U.S.A. report similar experiences and also similar vulnerabilities.

Evangelicals in mainline Protestant denominations face three awesome challenges just now. I believe these challenges are, humanly speaking, on the way to becoming insuperable.

Challenge One

Evangelicals in mainline churches stand on sandy ground historically. They have never been fully welcomed nor have they ever felt unapprehensively comfortable in "liberal" churches. Evangelical Episcopalians are usually regarded in their own place as "fundamentalists" beamed down from another planet. While I may consider myself and my colleagues the true "core Anglican," standing on Scripture and the official formularies of Anglican Christianity, specifically the Thirty-nine Articles of the Church of England, our Reformation confession, many in my church regard me as an alien virus. This is not paranoia. Many, especially those in the hierarchy, do not conceive how it could be that classic evangelicalism and classic Episcopalianism can really have anything in common. I mean, is not the Episcopal Church the very place of refuge to which burned-over and appalled *former* evangelicals flee? Together with a few former Roman Catholic priests who wished to marry?

Evangelicals in mainline churches have an "image" problem which is very hard to correct, especially given the ignorance of church history on the part of most laity, not to mention clergy.

People often ask me, "Why do you stay in the Episcopal Church? Your concerns seem more appropriate to the Presbyterian Church in America or the Lutheran Church–Missouri Synod." If I tell them about John Jewel or Charles Simeon or even John Stott, I might as well be speaking Hebrew.

Challenge Two

Evangelical clergy in mainline churches are having a very hard time reproducing ourselves. There are few distinctly evangelical seminaries that are directly sponsored by mainline jurisdictions. Evangelical Methodists go to Asbury—but is Asbury fully kosher? Evangelical Presbyterians go to . . . well, where do they go? They tend to go to non-PCUSA schools like Westminster or RTS (Reformed Theological Seminary) or to interdenominational schools like Fuller. But then getting ordained becomes a problem. It is no good spending three years at Regent College or Beeson Divinity School or Gordon-Conwell if you cannot get your driving license at the end of it all.

In my own denomination, we have struggled to establish an evangelical seminary, Trinity School for Ministry, in Ambridge, Pennsylvania. But very, very few bishops will allow candidates for holy orders to attend our school. Most bishops say we are "biblicist" or "fundamentalist" or "narrow." The result is that evangelically inclined seminarians in (P)ECUSA are not free to be trained where they wish to be and where their sponsoring parishes wish them to be. So people like me cannot reproduce ourselves.

Now, we could encourage young men and women to go where they feel called to go *anyway*. And we do. But it becomes extremely hard to get such people ordained. In liturgical churches, and even in historically Word-centered churches such as the Reformed, renewal has almost always occurred as the result of renewed *clergy*. Our old liturgical churches are not able to sustain laity-led renewal movements. Yes, for a time, lay movements like the 1970s charismatic renewal could do great and transformative things. But in the long run, the spiritual health of the ordained clergy is key for us. Thus when we feel we are being blocked from reproducing ourselves, our hopes for the future sink like lead.

Challenge Three

The same interest in *ecclesiology* that has grown so dramatically in evangelical circles within the last twenty years has grown equally as strong in the mainline churches. Not only has this meant an increasingly "high" style of worship, a pervasive focus on liturgy, ritual, the "Holy Eucharist," and also on what I regard as liturgical kitsch, such as "blessings of the animals," labyrinths, house blessings, and so forth. The turn to ecclesiology has also involved a *centralizing* trend in the mainline denominations. By this I mean a palpable centering of power within the hierarchy. Evangelicals experience less and less "live and let live" in our old denominations.

Where once we could do our work more or less as we thought it should be done, without interference, as long as we stayed in our parishes and paid our assessments or church tax to the central authority, we now have bishops looking over our shoulder and harassing us. This is not overstated. My evangelical brothers and sisters with whom I have served for twenty and thirty years in the ministry all report that they are increasingly having to answer to bishops and boards and diocesan authorities.

I do not therefore observe that the turn to ecclesiology is an evangelical phenomenon solely. Even my colleagues in ministry in the Church of England report an increasingly centralized or bureaucratic model of church oversight.

A key word here, at least in Anglican circles—though I have heard it from Methodist bishops as well—is *collegiality*. Collegiality is the idea that bishops are responsible to each other in cadre, and that their unity, at least as seen from the outside, is a vital good. The notion that church ministry trumps apostolic truth is a watchword now, a commonly heard axiom at least among Episcopalians. Such a view destroys the primacy of gospel over church.

In fact, the view that "unity" overrides "truth" is what our blessed Reformers were called to contend against at the period of the Reformation. Evangelicals can never agree to the view that unity is more important than truth. Such a view dismantles everything we believe we are laboring to achieve.

Centralized church structures have never been an easy fit for evangelicals. Mostly, we have done the "minimum," chuckled about the pretensions of the rest of it, and just gone about our work. But this is becoming harder and harder to do.

Conclusion

The three challenges I have emphasized are the key ones for us in the early twenty-first century. I have not emphasized theological or cultural issues, about which we are also very concerned, such as active homosexuality among the clergy or weakened ideas concerning original sin, and thus enervated views of Jesus Christ. For us in the mainline, the killing fields are those related to control and reproduction. We cannot go on if our life's blood is choked off at the source! I regard the failure of the mainline denominations to allow for the training of evangelical ministers to be the root cause of declining clergy morale within my own denomination. I believe that many evangelical Methodists and Presbyterians, among others, would agree. I believe that unless recourse is found in respect to challenges two and three, they will become cyanide pills. Is there hope for mainstream evangelicals in the next decade? I do not know. If some true *statesmen* rise up and lead the mainline denominations, men and women who are able to give ground from the heart and not from expedience, some accommodation may be possible. But I cannot see any such statesmen on the horizon, nor do I see where they could possibly come from. At the same time, the exodus to more conservative groups continues. In my own denomination's case, the AMiA (Anglican Mission in America) is an attractive refuge for previously mainline Episcopalians who are evangelical. The trouble is, once an Episcopal priest leaves for the AMiA, he never, or very, very rarely, ever returns. This is a psychological phenomenon akin to divorce—you obliterate and "blacken" the bad one from whom you fled. These people never come back.

For my wife and myself, we would already have "gone out from amongst them" if (P)ECUSA were all we knew. But we studied in the Church of England, with evangelicals there who had embraced a very different approach to episcopal polity. Later we studied at Tübingen, where ideas, not form, drive the Christian enterprise.

Can we stay? So far all right. But I am not sanguine, in my flesh. We do believe in Christ the Savior. We do pray to God the Creator *ex nihilo*. We have seen the fruit and gifts of God the Holy Spirit. We love the Bible. We have some friends in our stream—though many have died or left, and even more have been dead for hundreds of years. What is the future? A christological one, that we know, that at the very least.

13

God Is Working among Us

Diane Knippers

A few years ago, there was an Episcopal priest named Scott who was an assistant pastor in a United Methodist church near Omaha, Nebraska. How he got that job is a story in itself, no doubt. He was serving in this United Methodist church when Jimmy Creech, another United Methodist pastor, performed a same-sex, so-called marriage in Omaha. This evangelical Episcopalian was shaken to the core. He was disturbed by the curious pattern he saw among other local pastors. Evangelical pastors were outspoken about their beliefs in their own congregations, but quiet beyond the local church. Liberals were silent about their beliefs in their own congregations, but outspoken beyond. Scott was conflicted and unsure what to do. After all, this was not even his denomination. Then he read an article about a Vietnamese pastor in a labor camp. This pastor's job in the camp was to shovel excrement. The pastor said he did that odious task while rejoicing in the Lord. This story of suffering convinced Scott—and he decided nobody would do anything that bad to him—so he began to speak up.

He spoke up in his congregation. He wrote letters and organized meetings and prayer rallies. He was not hateful or mean spirited, but stood for the truth. When appointment time came, Scott was assigned to a small rural church. His daughter was disabled and needed services found only in urban areas, how-

ever, and he could not take the appointment. He lost his job
and was unemployed for six months.

Praise God, the story does not end there. He began to worship in a nearby Episcopal parish. When my own church hired
the rector of that Iowa parish, Scott served as interim rector
and, after a search process, was named rector.

In this essay I want to communicate what I see happening in
our churches and in renewal. I want us to discern together
what God is doing in the church as we enter the twenty-first
century.

Renewal in the historic Protestant churches of North America is at an important juncture. Most of the current renewal organizations have emerged since the late sixties. Although born
out of conditions in church and in society in the late twentieth
century, the theological problems in our churches stem from
modernist trends that are much older. The leaders of these renewal groups are beginning to retire. Some of those founders
may have thought that a strong dose of publicity and a bit of organizing would solve the problems facing our churches. Those
hopes surely have been disappointed.

One important measure of the health of a church—membership statistics—shows our churches in continual decline. It is a
sad, but familiar, story. From 1990 to 2000, according to a
study released in September, the Evangelical Lutheran Church
in America declined 2.2 percent; the Episcopal Church declined 5.3 percent; the American Baptist churches declined 5.7
percent; the United Methodist Church declined 6.7 percent;
the Presbyterian Church (USA) declined 11.6 percent; and the
United Church of Christ declined a whopping 14.8 percent.
During this decade, the population of the United States increased by more than 13 percent.

In this same period, by and large, growing congregations
were more conservative—Southern Baptists, Assemblies of
God, the Roman Catholic Church, the Churches of Christ. The
Presbyterian Church in America grew by 42 percent and the
Wesleyan Church by about 47 percent. The growing churches
are attracting immigrants, younger people, the unchurched—
and, yes, some of the former members of mainline churches.

This surely suggests that the mainline is an increasingly ir-

relevant sideline. Let me, as an aside, illustrate this point of ir-
relevancy. Opposition to the war on terrorism, and to the war
on Iraq, has been the loudest message of our denominational
leaders for many months. It's perfectly legitimate for Christians to disagree on foreign policy. The problem with what our
church leaders have said and done is not their opposition to
military actions, but that they argued in histrionic, biased, ex-
aggerated, and irresponsible ways. And they are having no impact in Washington. None whatsoever. All of their resolutions
and statements and demonstrations are making no difference.
None.

Mainline churches are declining and increasingly irrelevant,
even on issues that are a top priority for church leaders. So, if
vibrant, healthy, growing denominations are the goal of our reform movement, we have not achieved success. We have not
yet accomplished our purpose, not achieved our aim.

So, do we press on?

The Confessing Theologians Commission has offered us a
powerful statement of encouragement, "Be Steadfast." This
document is included as an appendix to this volume. I am convinced that this challenge is exactly right.

Historians confirm this. When has the church not needed renewal and reform? There certainly are times of relative health
and revival and times of apostasy and dissolution in church
history. In our denominations, these are not good days. But
they are not the worst days in church history either.

Read the appalling stories of the papacy and church hierarchy during the Medici period, with its shocking materialistic
and sexual excesses. I don't think any of our denominations
match that era of church history in its breathtaking debauch-
ery. However, in contrast, study the life and ministry of the
current pope, John Paul II. We must quickly conclude that, yes,
reformations are possible—even *within* a church.

Too many contemporary Christians make the wrong assumptions about church renewal and reform. They confuse the
goal or the ideal with the norm. They think that the normal or
typical state of Christ's church is what it *ought* to be—unified,
holy, courageous, peaceful, charitable, teaching truth at all levels. Yet the church typically isn't like that.

In fact, the biblical and historical evidence is that it never has been that way. Church reform isn't some unusual tangent activity. It is the *normal* responsibility of those who love God. It is *integral* to God's redemptive project. We do not reform the church so that we can get on with the other tasks—mission, evangelism, discipleship, seeking justice and righteousness. No, church reform is part of the task of the church.

The early church was no golden age. The epistles are directed toward every kind of problem within the church, from the theological errors of Gnosticism, to instructions about social responsibility, to admonitions about sexual immorality. The church itself was plagued by immorality.

Or read about the early centuries of church history and the ecumenical councils. What incredible struggles! What gripping conflict! Lives were at stake; empires hung in the balance. Indeed, the orthodox faith of the church was in doubt.

These were theological, spiritual, and political battles. They make even the most serious theological conflicts in the contemporary church look almost tame. But out of the refining fire of those theological conflagrations have come precious gifts—including the Nicene Creed that is said weekly in churches around the world.

Reformation is simply one of the ongoing tasks of the church. We must look for the blessing of this work—that our most difficult battles may produce incredible gifts for our children's children.

If reform is a constant, what, then, are the attributes of our contemporary reform movements? What is God doing among us in this day? How can we discern God's work among us? I have identified six emerging characteristics of contemporary reformation.

Contemporary Reform Is Mature and Diverse

First, the renewing and confessing movement is mature and multifaceted. To be sure, some organizations are young—but they are joining a movement that has decades of experience.

Organizations are engaged in missions and in publishing, in strengthening theological education, in evangelism, and in church planting. We are engaged in microenterprise development and human rights advocacy. We are building marriages, defending the unborn, and healing the sexually broken. We are changing the tenor and results at the assemblies and conventions and conferences of our denominations.

Let me say a word about our diversity. Is all this diversity positive? Do we need this many organizations?

There must be cooperation within and between denominations. The task is too urgent to allow for petty bickering and competition. Having said that, our many and diverse organizations are a strength. They appeal to different gifts and callings. More groups can accommodate more people and more strategies and more outreach.

We don't need fewer reform groups, fewer renewal strategies, fewer committed leaders, fewer confessing movements. We need more. The United Methodist Foundation for Theological Education should be duplicated in other denominations. The high circulation and aggressive reporting of *The Presbyterian Layman* and *United Methodist Action* should be replicated in the Episcopal Church and the Evangelical Lutheran Church in America. The global antipoverty work of the Anglican Five Talents organization should be emulated by others. Every denomination needs a group parallel to a new Presbyterian group I've just learned about called Youth For Truth. We are a mature and diverse movement.

Contemporary Reform Is Ecumenical

Our renewing and confessing movement is ecumenical. One of the first charges against the Institute on Religion and Democracy in the early 1980s was one of anti-ecumenicalism. The accusation, of course, stemmed from our forthright critique of the World Council of Churches and the National Council of Churches. Yet our board of directors is one of the most ecumenical boards in North America. Regarding ecumenism, our renewing and confessing movement is saying enough is enough. We will no longer allow an out-of-touch and declining organization such as the National Council of Churches, representing less than one-third of American Christians, to claim the mantle of Christian unity.

We embrace ecumenism. We know that Christian unity can

only be found in Truth—the truth of our Lord and Savior Jesus Christ. We watch with anticipation to see God's work in unifying his church—recognizing that unity is God's gift, not a construct of committees and commissions. The third Christian millennium is bringing the promise of a new ecumenism. We are committed to this new ecumenism.

Let me say one more word about ecumenism and church reform. The reformation we seek will not come to just one denomination. When I prayerfully consider the renewal we seek, I can't even imagine that the Presbyterians would experience some kind of dramatic change that would pass the Methodists by. How could there be a reformation that would touch one denomination and bypass another?

Let's be very clear about what we really desire, hope for, contend for, and pray for. Let's be really clear about what we need. Reformation is more than making minor changes in church canons or adopting biblically based petitions or even electing orthodox leaders. Our plight is too serious for that. We need revival. We yearn for another Great Awakening. The Holy Spirit doesn't bring Great Awakenings to denominations. He brings them to cities, to regions, and, please God, to our nations.

Contemporary Reform Is Theological

There are others more able, but I must say just a word or two about theology. First, let me note simply that the renewing and confessing movement is theologically serious. One of our group publishes a journal titled simply *Theology Matters.* It's perhaps no coincidence that this orthodox Presbyterian publication was launched by Sue Cyre, who did major reporting on the first Re-imagining Conference.

Through our debates with revisionist theologies, we are rediscovering and reembracing our heritage. We are studying and reaffirming and reasserting the atonement, the incarnation, and the bodily resurrection. We don't take these for granted. We study patristics. We no longer mumble our way through the creeds, we proclaim them. We savor their truth and beauty.

Our movement is fully trinitarian. We worship God the Father, God the Son, and God the Holy Spirit, knowing that to neglect any person of the Trinity is to distort the gospel and leave ourselves bereft of God's full power and blessing.

Theologically, we are at a challenging historical moment as we move from modernity to postmodernity. For years, we have struggled with the modernists—those sons and daughters of the Enlightenment, marked by rationalism and materialism, dismissive of miracles, and alienated from the transcendent. Admittedly, these often-aging voices receive media attention and adulation in some circles. We Episcopalians are rightly embarrassed that the most well-known Episcopal bishop in the country is John Shelby Spong.

But we must not waste too much time and energy combating worn-out and unappealing modernist heresies. We face new, insidious challenges. In a postmodern era, the problem may not be unbelief, but too much belief—belief in anything and everything. Donna Hailson calls it cafeteria religion—where people create their own religion piecemeal out of the beliefs and practices of a global cornucopia of options. Here, the radical feminist theologians lead the way—mixing Wiccan crowning ceremonies, Eastern healing rituals, erotic litanies, drums and chants invoking ancestors, and even some old camp-meeting hymns—all in an intoxicating, poisonous brew. Our postmodernist challenge is to answer not those who believe too little, but those who will believe everything. Theology matters, indeed, now more than ever.

Contemporary Reform Addresses Moral Concerns

Our renewing and confessing movement confronts a deepening apologetic task—not just about theology, but also in ethics. We must address contemporary moral and social issues. This is a direct product of the dramatic changes in our society.

When I first went to work at *Good News* magazine nearly thirty years ago, it usually was enough to report that some church leader was endorsing homosexual practice. Readers immediately would grasp the problem.

In just a few decades, the moral climate of the West has dramatically shifted. The simple proposition that sexual intercourse ought to be reserved for lifelong marriage between one man and one woman is contested, in word and deed, on every side. It's not enough to report what is wrong in our churches, we have to teach why it is wrong.

As in every age there is a need for church reform. Reform movements rise up in reaction to what is wrong, to false teaching and evil practice. But the result can be a great blessing to the church universal as we affirm what is good and right and true.

The reform battles of the early church gave us the blessing of creedal affirmations of Christ's humanity and divinity. The monastic reforms have left a legacy of spiritual disciplines that grace our lives. Men of courage and conviction were martyred so that we might read of the Holy Scripture in our own language. The great proclamation of justification by faith—which we now hear echoing throughout the universal church—sprang from the lips of Reformers challenging a church in which it seemed that everything could be bought.

Some of the deepest wrongs we face today have to do with human sexuality—the abuse and misuse of one of God's greatest gifts. In the midst of current struggles, we may miss a larger redemptive possibility. I am convinced that God will use this struggle to rejuvenate and redeem marriage. My own marriage has been immeasurably strengthened as I've struggled with the issues we face and studied to find answers in natural law, in tradition, and in Scripture. I see so many young marriages that benefit from the intentional determination of men and women to form godly unions in opposition to cultural pressures.

We are all discouraged from time to time. Whether flipping channels on television or listening to the debate in the House of Bishops, my anguished cry is often, "What are we coming to? Where will it end? How far can this go?"

But history teaches and faith assures this: Out of this deep and terrible struggle, God will reveal more to us about what he intended all along for marriage than any generation has ever known before.

Marriage and sexuality are not the only issues demanding a new apologetic today. Another great moral struggle today is over life itself. When does life begin? When does it end? Who decides?

The renewing and confessing movements have strong orga-

nizations fighting the scourge of abortion and seeking to protect children and women from this great social evil. We are not
yet equipped and ready to face the end-of-life questions. Partly
this is because our churches are not taking uniform and pre-
dictable positions on euthanasia, assisted suicide, stem-cell research, cloning, and so on. There is not a lot of truly bad teaching coming from our churches on these issues, demanding our
reaction. But there's not a lot of teaching on these issues from
the churches, period.

This is an area in which the renewing and confessing movement can and should lead. We need researchers and writers, we
need task forces and models of ministry. We need to do this
now.

This is more than a theoretical issue—more than an ethical
or political debate. As baby boomers age and as life expectan-
cies increase, the care of the elderly will become a critical national issue. There will be increased pressure on the aged and
infirm to end their own lives—pressure often consistent with
their own desire to die rather than lose independence.

The question over the worth of the human person will be
asked, not just at the beginning of life, but increasingly to the
end. The struggle will play out in our homes and communities.
We need families and congregations willing to testify to the in-
finite worth of each person created in God's image by their sacrificial service to those nearing the end of life.

Then there are the character issues in our corporate and economic life. Greed, deception, and corruption—all personal
moral failings whatever else they are—have severely damaged
our economic institutions. Even worse, they have betrayed the
promise of free economies to those escaping communism and
to the poorest of the poor around the globe.

Another moral issue has to do with our popular culture and
media and their saturation with debased sexual images. So
much of our entertainment is squalid and dehumanizing. Yes,
its victims certainly are women and children, but men as well.
The Internet makes all of this even more insidious.

I would like to see our church leaders spend as much time
clamoring for change in the media as they do in governments.
United Methodist bishops demonstrated in front of the White
House. Why don't they demonstrate in front of motion-picture

studios or the corporate offices of Internet providers? What if our church activists and social-action agencies organized letter-writing crusades and divestment campaigns and petitions and resolutions and turn-off-the-television weeks—all aimed at purveyors of pornography and unending sex and violence in our entertainment industry?

Washington and Ottawa may be the political capitals of our two nations, but New York and Hollywood are the media capitals of the world. It wouldn't even require a huge ideological or theological shift for our churches to lead this kind of effort. It really only requires the will and the effort. This is something our renewal groups could lead.

Again, we see the connection between a moral failure in the West and its negative impact throughout the world. The popular culture that we export discredits democracy and human freedom and, to the degree that our nations are identified as Christian, our faith. So, both the blessing of liberty and the glorious hope of the Christian gospel are tarnished by the media images we broadcast around the world. The most serious price for this often is paid by the most vulnerable—for example, Christian minorities in Islamic-dominated lands.

This leads me to a final emerging issue I want to highlight. We have a huge apologetic task in the face of the rise of Islam—including challenging the shocking myopia and naïveté of many of our church leaders before this threat.

We see on the part of many of our church leaders a reprise of the kind of response they made to totalitarian communism two decades ago. The Soviets, like many Muslim nations today, were abusive of basic human rights, including religious freedom. There was the constant threat of armed conflict—including terrifying unconventional weapons. Too often, church leaders felt that their peace advocacy required denying the human rights abuses.

Today, Islam is portrayed as an innocuous, peaceful religion. The existence of a radical Islam is minimized or denied. We are well on our way to betraying Christians, Jews, and even moderate Muslims who are minorities in Islamic regimes—just as we so scandalously betrayed fellow Christians in the Soviet empire.

This is an issue in which the renewing and confessing movement can be on the side of democracy, human rights, religious rights, and the rights of women. This is an issue about which we can remind the leaders of the mainline churches that there ultimately can be no peace, unless there also is justice.

Contemporary Reform Is Global

The reform movement is a global movement—and must become even more so. We Anglicans recognize how much we need the witness of the growing body of Anglicans in the Global South. We see our mutual dependence—the churches of Africa, Latin America, and Asia need our resources, our technology. They need enormous help in countering poverty, in combating AIDS, and in building just and free societies. They need help with theological training to provide pastors for all the new converts. But we have realized how much we need them as well. We need their fervency, their gospel commitment, their evangelistic zeal, their towering faith.

But this connection is not only for Anglicans, it is for all of us. The center of Christendom has moved south. Most mainline churches are connected to world movements such as the World Methodist Council, the Baptist World Alliance, and so on. Our reform movements must build a relationship of mutual service and support with like-minded believers through such global movements where possible, and around them as necessary.

There is an irony of our time. We are more aware than ever of the fact that around the globe our brothers and sisters in Christ are suffering and dying for the faith. They suffer for the same faith that many of our church leaders are undermining and that too many of us are too timid to defend.

There is unity in suffering. What if God is using the suffering of the persecuted church to embolden us? Would he allow their suffering to teach me something about him and defend his truth? Nothing has humbled me more than to make that connection.

Some American church leaders are reimagining, distorting, demeaning, and denying the very faith for which some Christians in our world are dying. Our brothers and sisters are suffering slavery, hunger, oppression, and imprisonment—and some are shoveling excrement—to defend the gospel. My dear friends, we may feel the sting of prejudice and marginalization in our churches, but we have not yet begun to suffer for the faith.

Contemporary Reform Is Generational

In our renewing and confessing movement God is raising up a new generation of reformers. God is renewing his church, but it is a multigenerational project. Let me tell you what I am convinced God is doing. He is raising up a new generation to be Athanasius.

I want to tell you about Melissa Bixler and Bruce Mason. When she still was in high school, Melissa went with me to the Episcopal General Convention and single-handedly organized other youths to testify on youth abstinence. When he was the assistant to the rector of a large church, Bruce spent the better part of a summer drafting a program of action for reforming the Episcopal Church—and now works for the American Anglican Council.

Some of these young reformers are on the staff of our Institute on Religion and Democracy, such as Jerald Walz. Last spring, Jerald was a lay delegate to his United Methodist annual conference, where he gave major impetus to an effort to see that an ordained man who had a sex-change operation did not receive an appointment. Meghan Furlong helped recruit a team of nearly a dozen members of her church to attend this conference, including four other young adults. I can't forget when Steve Rempe came back from a general assembly of the Evangelical Lutheran Church in America and told of going to report on a press conference organized by homosexuals—and recognized that he was the only straight person in the room. Most recently, he and one of his colleagues braved a World Council of Churches– and National Council of Churches-sponsored conference in Washington, D.C., prepared a sharply critical and insightful report on its excesses, and engaged in a spirited correspondence with some of the conference leaders.

Why do I think these young reformers follow in the steps of Athanasius? They are young and energetic. They are respectful, but they are not willing to leave the important task of reform to their elders or to those who outrank them in the church. If the bishops can't or won't be apologists for the gospel, they will. They are articulate and eloquent defenders of the faith. They are thoughtful, and they do their homework. They are not silent. They know that they well may spend their lives in ecclesiastical exile. Their goal isn't a comfortable career or high church office. Their evangelical parents and grandparents often were shocked to discover the heresies and injustices of our denominations, but this generation knows what it is getting into. They are not looking for material success, nor for ecclesiastical security and comfort. If they wanted the latter, they could find more amenable denominations or start an independent congregation. But they are accepting God's call to join the movement for reformation. They are prepared for exile.

Conclusion

What is the future of the church? What is the future of our movement?

I do not have the gift of prophecy. All I can do is study our history, observe the work of the Holy Spirit in our midst, and claim the promises of God for our future.

I do not think the shape of the future church will be the bureaucratic, politicized, modernist denominations of the twentieth century. In fact, I believe the church will be mature and diverse, ecumenical, theologically grounded, capable of addressing major ethical issues, and global, and it will be shaped and lived by the next generation. The church will change. God will not. I do know one thing about the future—it will be a future in which God keeps his promises.

A couple of Sundays ago, my good United Methodist friends, John and Helen Rhea Stumbo, were visiting my husband and me in Washington and came to our Episcopal church with us. Our closing hymn was one of my favorites, "The Church's One Foundation Is Jesus Christ Her Lord." As we sang the final notes, I turned and saw tears in Helen's eyes. "We don't have that third verse in our hymnal," she said. "And it so spoke to me and what I've been wrestling with."

Consider these words:

> Though with a scornful wonder men see her sore oppressed,
> By schisms rent asunder, by heresies distressed;

> Yet saints their watch are keeping, their cry goes up "How
>   long?"
> And soon the night of weeping shall be the morn of song.

For two thousand years the saints and martyrs have cried,
"How long?" Today, across the globe, our suffering brothers
and sisters cry, "How long?" I have wept tears outside the
House of Bishops and cried, "How long?"

We cling to the promise that soon, soon, soon, the night of
weeping shall be the morn of song.

14

Renewal in the Mainline

An Evangelical Outsider's Perspective

John H. Armstrong

The sawdust trail brings back poignant personal memories. Though I never actually walked a sawdust trail, my early Christian faith was nurtured in a context that had close religious and social ties to the trail. Spring and fall revival meetings linger in my mind to this day, memories of nightly meetings filled with gospel songs and fervent sermons appealing for personal trust in Christ.

But what does this have to do with mainline churches? When did anyone think of the sawdust trail in association with the United Church of Christ? What about the United Methodists, that grand expression of piety from the eighteenth-century evangelical revivals? And what about the Episcopal Church, the Disciples of Christ, the American Baptists, the Presbyterian Church (U.S.A.), and the Evangelical Lutheran Church in America? I have found that many evangelical Christians are surprised to hear that God is doing something new and fresh in these mainline churches. The story is one that needs to be told much more widely, for God is at work doing a "new thing."

As an evangelical from outside the mainline, I confess that my personal perspective was very limited until I began to meet hungering and thirsting ordinary folks from mainline churches.

This journey began several years ago. My perspective, prior to seeing what is happening firsthand, was formed much more by politics and public debates than from actual experience and careful research. Now, as a very interested friend of renewal and reformation, I stand amazed at the theological vigor, spiritual life, and social awareness of evangelical faith and practice from within the mainline. I have seen historic church bodies experience the rising tide of ministers and lay leadership standing firmly for the gospel of Christ, against both pluralism and ethical compromise. And I note, with some degree of optimism, that the latest Gallup audit of denominational preferences reveals a leveling out, and even an upturn, in the strength of certain mainline denominations after decades of numerical loss.[1]

My journey really began as a college student in 1970. The fires of revival were experienced in the Jesus movement and on college campuses across the nation. My life had been touched deeply. I earnestly began to study the historic patterns of spiritual renewal. I saw how churches in history often declined in membership, orthodox confession, and spiritual life. I also saw that God periodically intervened to rescue churches and Christian schools and institutions by the effectual work of the Holy Spirit breathing new life into multitudes of people. My more conservative and separatist background generally insisted that older declining denominations would never be rescued, thus the faithful should abandon them to the liberals. I can remember being asked more than once, "Can you give me one example of a denomination or church body that moved down the road to apostasy that ever came back?" Well, the last twenty years have provided several outstanding examples that actually prove this thesis suspect. I submit that the next twenty might show even more astounding outcomes if the renewal leadership of the mainline denominations is successful.

A Brief History

There are dozens of identifiable renewal groups scattered throughout the older denominations in North America. These groups, small and large, go by many names. Some have extensive staff, fairly large budgets, and widely read publications. Others are smaller and are led by a handful of active, prayerful, sacrificial ministers and laypeople. They range from small groups like Biblical Witness Fellowship (United Church of Christ), American Baptist Evangelicals, Disciples Heritage Fellowship (Disciples of Christ), and Episcopalians United (Episcopal Church, U.S.A.), to the older and larger Good News Fellowship (United Methodist), Presbyterian Lay Committee, and Presbyterians for Renewal (PCUSA). A good example of the way such renewal groups envision themselves is seen in the story of Presbyterians for Renewal (PFR). This group, organized in 1989, clearly states that its mission "is to participate in God's renewing, transforming work in the Presbyterian Church." PFR openly says that it wants to renew the churches and people of their denomination by rooting their values in submission to the Lordship of Jesus Christ. To do this, PFR's vision statement says that they will anchor all efforts in God's Word and the historic Reformed faith. In addition, their vision statement adds that PFR will be passionate about shaping the church's life and theology, positively engage the structure and politics of the denomination, seek to work with others who share their mission, serve in ways that reflect the graciousness of Christ, and pray with dependence upon God's direction and power.

This type of statement is somewhat typical of the growing renewal groups in the mainline churches. Some are more aggressive in confronting particular issues in their denominations while others seem to take a more low-key approach. All express commitment to stay in, and to pray and work for change. The goal for all seems to be something like this—work for reformation and pray for renewal by the Holy Spirit. This is also expressed well in the introduction to the Web site of Good News, a United Methodist renewal movement: "For more than thirty-four years Good News has been a voice for evangelical and historic Wesleyan concerns in our church. We are committed to being a voice for repentance, an agent for reform, and a catalyst for renewal within our denomination." Note the emphasis in the several key words used here: "a voice for repentance," and "an agent for reform." Further, the movement expresses the desire to be "a catalyst for renewal within our denomination." Every group I have examined states almost exactly the same goal.

What Happened?

Many events coalesced in the 1960s and '70s to prompt the rise of most of these burgeoning and highly influential grassroots renewal movements. Especially interesting is the story of Parker T. Williamson, a PCUSA minister who serves as chief operating officer for the thirty-two-year-old Presbyterian Lay Committee and as executive editor for *The Layman,* a publication sent to more than 575,000 households every month.

Early in his career, Parker Williamson was pastor of the six-hundred-member First Presbyterian Church in Lenoir, North Carolina. He was also a rising leader in his denomination and a member of the General Assembly Mission Board of the Presbyterian Church, U.S. (PCUS), as the Southern church was called before the reunion of North and South into the PCUSA. Then a defining moment came which thrust him into the middle of renewal efforts in the wider Presbyterian Church. Williamson was a hunger-program activist for the PCUS mission board who went from church to church raising money for food and technical assistance for churches in Third World settings. The money he was raising was channeled to the Presbyterian board. Williamson would learn sometime later that money he had raised, which went from the Presbyterian board to the World Council of Churches, had been used to finance guerilla warfare under the guise of "attacking hunger's root causes." When Williamson read of Rhodesian guerrillas shooting down a mission plane and killing the believers on board, he realized that he had, in effect, helped to fund the very guerrillas who had killed fellow Christians. He says, upon learning this: "I went ballistic. I felt I had betrayed Presbyterians by my participation in that program." Sometime later Williamson began his relentless efforts to expose the denomination's compromises, including its support of liberation theology. As a result of these efforts the mission now receives nearly 74 percent of its funds as donor-directed gifts. By this means the monies will not be used for political causes that are offensive to evangelical donors.

Williamson is, in many ways, a prototypical renewal leader in the mainline. He was one of three students from Union Theological Seminary to join Martin Luther King in his march to Selma, Alabama, in the 1960s. As a young minister in North

Carolina he developed a biracial community of 140 privately owned homes for people with low to moderate incomes by leading an all-white church to get financially involved in the effort. Williamson demonstrates his aggressive challenge to the establishment leadership of his own church by saying:

> They talk a big game about community involvement. But I find that they are rarely involved personally. Often they use the church to lobby for government programs whose effectiveness in meeting human needs is not at all clear. It has been my observation that people who take the Scriptures seriously go into the streets, roll up their sleeves and work for and with the poor. You can't read the Scriptures and not be involved.[2]

Today, many years later, the energetic and visionary Parker Williamson travels extensively across his denomination working for biblical and theological renewal in the Presbyterian Church U.S.A. He likes to speak about the wind as the metaphor for God's Spirit blowing across the church in dark times, leading his people back to repentance and faith. He writes, "You can defy bullets, bombs, bad theology and the words of scoffers, but not the breath of God."[3]

The Issues

Perhaps no single issue galvanized the evangelical renewal movement in the mainline churches quite like the Re-imagining Conference, an event held in Minneapolis in the mid-1990s that was devoted to worshiping God as Sophia. It was widely sponsored by a number of mainline groups. Church funding for this gathering was reported in the media, both print and television. The issue got massive attention and has been discussed since. It seems to have awakened a sleeping giant in some quarters. Laypeople began to sense that something radically different was going on in their churches.

Just as liberation theology had awakened Parker Williamson some years prior to the goddess movement, the aggressive promotion of practicing homosexuals as members and ministers lit a new fire. This issue has drawn even more interest in renewing denominations that once stood as the very definition of ethical and moral stability.

But it would be a mistake to think that all these movements are about is social and ethical change. The goal is clearly much bigger. Thousands of ministers and lay leaders now see that their historic agencies and institutions are in need of a theological blood transfusion. They realize that much more than stopping a few votes in presbyteries, general assemblies, and conferences is needed. They want to go back to their historic foundations and root the present and future in the past. They want to remind their respective churches that they really do believe something definitive and they need to recover this and experience afresh the winds of God's Spirit blowing upon their people.

The Association for Church Renewal

When I first learned of various mainline renewal movements I was surprised and pleased to discover, through the kindness of James V. Heidinger II (Good News, United Methodist Church), that there was a genuine ecumenism of the trenches among those who work and pray for renewal in their respective church bodies. The Association for Church Renewal (ACR) is an association of executives and leaders of more than thirty church renewal organizations and ministries that are related to mainline denominations in both the United States and Canada. Its founding purpose statement is: "An association to encourage and support renewal and reform leaders from the 'mainline' denominations, assisting them in developing their ministries' witness to orthodox Christianity in both church and society."[4]

This group of renewal leaders began to meet in 1979 to pray together and to give mutual encouragement and support. A few years ago the group decided to become more than an ad hoc gathering and formed an official organization in October 1996. These leaders believe that there is far more orthodox and evangelical faith to be found in the mainline than the program and public statements of denomination leaders would indicate. James Heidinger notes that one survey shows that within United Methodism alone more than 70 percent of the members believed the Bible to be the Word of God without error. Heidinger, and many of his fellow renewal leaders, also believe that most of the churches from the Two-Thirds World constituency of the World Council of Churches are both orthodox and evangelically vibrant. This explains why the most recent Lambeth Conference of the Anglican communion spoke so clearly about issues of biblical fidelity, much to the chagrin of liberal leaders such as John Shelby Spong and others.

As a result of these observations the ACR sought to have a presence at the World Council of Churches meeting at Harare, Zimbabwe, December 3–14, 1998. Their effort led them to produce a document, *Jubilee Appeal*, with position papers on seven major issues facing the World Council of Churches. The *Jubilee Appeal* seeks to present a biblical perspective on issues such as syncretism, revisionism, and "re-imagining" the faith. Thomas C. Oden, a United Methodist theologian and professor at Drew University, chaired the Jubilee Project. Diane Knippers, vice-chair of the ACR and president of The Institute on Religion and Democracy, called the *Jubilee Appeal* "a 'Macedonia call' to the rest of the world—come over and help North America. We need missionary outreach to renew our own societies and to reform the WCC."[5]

The Failed Ecumenism

The National Council of Churches (NCC), representing thirty-six mostly Protestant denominations, appears to be a half-century experiment on the brink of failure. Not only does crippling debt threaten its future, but the failure to attract either Roman Catholics or evangelicals into its fold weighs against its ability to sustain long-term meaning. Its many unpopular decisions, often reflecting a leftist political and social agenda, have caused multitudes to hold it in deep suspicion. At the same time the National Association of Evangelicals (NAE), which was begun as an alternative movement to the NCC for evangelical churches and denominations, is facing rough waters of its own. Many seem to have drawn the conclusion that ecumenism is dead. Before the corpse is buried, it might be worth thinking about what is really happening at the grassroots.

The kind of ecumenism that has been at the forefront of

American Protestantism for more than fifty years is in trouble, even if the organizations can sustain some form of existence. At the same time, a new ecumenism, one self-consciously rooted in historically catholic, confessional, and evangelical theology, is growing without support from the recognized leadership of the ecumenical movement. This informal development is seen in ad hoc committees, developing agencies, college and seminary lecture series, and major conferences. It is here that my own journey intersects with the evangelical renewal going on in the mainline.

In 1991, several Chicago-area friends began Reformation & Revival Ministries to support a vision for restoring biblical concerns to the church and to pray for God-sent revival. At the time we only envisioned doing this by means of our quarterly publication, *Reformation and Revival Journal*. We were all members of self-consciously evangelical churches with backgrounds rooted in the movement. At the same time, we wanted to be open to what God was doing and to respond to where we saw the Spirit at work. None of us, at least in 1991, had any idea of how our vision would intersect with the mainline renewal groups I have described. During the past decade we sought to make friends for the gospel wherever possible. One such relationship was a developing friendship I had personally established with United Church of Christ theologian Donald G. Bloesch, who taught theology for more than thirty years at the University of Dubuque Theological Seminary (PCUSA). Dr. Bloesch is well known for his lifetime contribution to a centrist evangelical theological renewal. He has championed a theology of "Word and Spirit," central to the theological recovery of the sixteenth-century Protestant Reformation, without the more divisive elements of fundamentalism that so many of us knew firsthand. He has consistently affirmed orthodoxy while remaining open to learn from all traditions. He has remained focused upon Christ without accepting the more rationalistic elements of twentieth-century evangelicalism.

Through the concern of Dr. Bloesch, for both his former students and his own denomination, I heard about people that I didn't even know existed. I saw evidence that God was at work in a much wider way than I could have imagined, especially given my very conservative background. In 1998, we began to talk about holding a renewal conference for mainline leaders and laity on the campus of the University of Dubuque. Plenary speakers included well-known theologians like William Abraham (Methodist), Carl Braaten (Lutheran), James I. Packer (Anglican), and Donald Bloesch. People like Parker Williamson, James Heidinger, Todd Wetzel, David Runnion-Bareford, Peter Moore, Mark Achtemeier, Susan Cyre, Terry Schlossberg, and Helen Hitchcock made presentations on issues of concern to renewing the church. The spirit of the group was amazing. We experienced wonderful worship and fervent prayer joined with intellectual discussion. Without realizing the implications of this event, I found myself in the middle of a work of God that I had only recently come to know anything about.

In May 2001, we had a second "Word and Spirit" renewal event in Dubuque. The theme was evangelism, and the conference again proved to be a great joy. People from diverse backgrounds came together to learn, grow, and worship. The result has been a whole circle of new friends across many denominational distinctives. No one was asked to give up his or her doctrinal distinctives. Indeed our distinctives were the basis for much good discussion. Renewal groups caucused for times of discussion and prayer.

I can testify to the simple fact that something is happening in many churches in the old mainline groups. I have no idea how big this movement is, but it is increasingly taking shape and has life given by the Holy Spirit. It may not take form beyond its present informal network, but it has already produced evidence that God is not done with churches that many of us thought might be in the throes of ecclesiastical death.

Conclusion

As an outsider to all of this activity, and as one for whom the sawdust trail has special meaning, I must say that I see a growing fire among my mainline brothers and sisters in Christ. Will this fire grow and become a fully developed revival in the mainline churches? God alone knows the answer. It is not for us to know what the future holds, but we can look ahead with hope that the one who does know loves the church and revives it when and where he pleases. With the psalmist we can pray, whether we are believers in the mainline or not, "Will you not revive us again, that your people may rejoice in you?" (Ps. 85:6).

Appendix

Be Steadfast

A LETTER TO CONFESSING CHRISTIANS

Editor's Note: The Confessing Theologians Commission, a group of prominent theologians from most all of the mainline Protestant denominations in North America, met in Dallas, Texas, on September 20–22, 2002. The commission gathered at the invitation of Dr. Thomas Oden of Drew University, who called the group together under the auspices of the Association for Church Renewal (ACR). The following document, "Be Steadfast: A Letter to Confessing Christians," was developed by the Confessing Theologians Commission for the Confessing the Faith Conference. It is their response to three urgent questions put to them by the Association for Church Renewal.

God's solid foundation stands firm, sealed with this inscription: "The Lord knows those who are his," and, "Everyone who confesses the name of the Lord must turn away from wickedness."

—2 Timothy 2:19

Sisters and brothers in the Lord:

God alone renews and continues to bless his people. God has not abandoned his church, and calls us to keep faith with him and those dear to him. We are called to be obedient to the faith once for all delivered to the saints.

In thanksgiving for God's promises fulfilled in Jesus Christ, we seek to humble ourselves before him, pray, seek his face, and turn from sin, that he may hear, forgive, and heal. We all stand under divine judgment; we all are in need of divine grace. We give thanks also for this, the first North American gathering of renewing and confessing movements. Your conveners have asked confessing theologians to address three urgent questions facing all mainline renewal movements.

- Why should we remain in our churches?
- Why do our churches need faithful confessors?
- Why does our society need faithful Christian confessors?

1. Why should we remain in our churches?

The challenges facing our churches today are indeed immense. We have all seen declines in biblical and theological literacy, catechesis, and spiritual formation. Our churches have experienced severe declines in numbers of congregations and in absolute numbers of members. We have also seen our church rent by contentious argument, exhausted by never-ending conflict. Many grow weary, and wonder if they and their congregations should stay.

Our own experience speaks to this question, too. We have all passed through long seasons of anguish and travail, and we anticipate more. We are still here. The Holy Spirit has not abandoned our churches, neither will we.

Resignation, quietism, and despair do not serve the church catholic and the communion of saints. We urge our brothers and sisters not to withdraw, but mutually to encourage one another to a struggle in which there is good hope. Our Lord reminds us, "God removes every branch in me that bears no fruit. Every branch that bears fruit, he prunes to make it bear more fruit" (John 15:2). We pray God will give us courage, perseverance, and mettle for the task.

Much work has been begun by the various renewal movements among our churches. We note with thanksgiving the revival of Bible study, renewed interest in evangelization, fresh seasons of prayer, and renewed concern with the plight of the poor. We have committed ourselves to the ongoing life of the churches in which God has placed us, and we pledge our best efforts as theologians of the church to those who are engaged in this divine work of reform and renewal.

It is a beginning, and must continue, commending ourselves and our denominational leadership to God with fear and trembling.

But ultimately the reason we cannot and must not leave our denominations is that the Gospel can still be freely proclaimed in them and the sacraments administered without hindrance. However true it may be that "other gospels" are also heard in our midst, none of our churches have legislated against the preaching of the gospel of Jesus Christ. In such a situation, it is unnecessary for congregations to turn their backs on their churches.

2. Why do our churches need faithful confessors?

Churches need faithful confessors for one essential reason: a church that is unable to confess its faith is a lame and withered church. The church needs faithful witnesses in order to be the church of Jesus Christ.

We believe that God's call to be faithful witnesses within the churches requires not only truthful confession, but also a long-term effort to reform our institutions. Our deliberative, legislative, administrative, and educational structures in many instances do not faithfully serve the church's mission and pastoral obligations. The work and witness of faithful confessors helps to reclaim and redirect these institutions toward their proper ends. We, therefore, believe that confessing movements are necessary if the institutional forms of our churches are to be tied to God's purposes for his church.

We note with joy how renewal movements in many churches have led to the discovery of a common bond in the faith of the church catholic and mutual encouragement in the gospel. Across the renewal movements, we rejoice in the recovery of sound doctrine, for example the doctrine of the Trinity, and the doctrine of the unique, saving significance of Christ's person and work. God has enabled many to recover their intellectual nerve.

God has also blessed our churches in other ways through the work of the renewal movements. In some quarters, we see fresh vitality in worship and in preaching. In other quarters, we witness new ventures in mission, the renewal of personal piety, and an increase in enthusiastic discipleship. In still other places we see increased reading of Holy Scripture, deepened petitionary prayer, and a more profound embrace of God's concern for the poor.

God has given us a spirit of repentance and shed abroad his love afresh in our hearts. We expect further blessings in the years ahead, and we anticipate that God will continue to use renewal movements for the sustaining and furtherance of such blessings.

3. Why does our society need faithful Christian confessors?

Faithful Christian witness humanizes society and heals the nations. St. Paul teaches, echoing Isaiah, "The root of Jesse shall come, one who rises to rule the Gentiles; in him the Gentiles shall hope" (Rom. 15:12). Confessing Christ requires the discipline of life, personal and corporate, private and public.

In the absence of faithful Christian witness, society establishes false idols. The twentieth century is littered with the victims of secular ideology. Nazi and Marxist ideologies produced Auschwitz and the Gulag. The North American threat comes from a more benign form of atheism that banishes Christian witness from the public square. Consumerism, materialism, individualism, and hedonism rush in to fill the void. Dogmatic atheism brutalizes and destroys the church. The more benign and civil atheism seduces and marginalizes the church. Disoriented by the ideology of moral relativism, some church leaders haphazardly champion fashionable causes. In each case, the savor of the church and the light of Christ is lost.

In the mercy and power of God, a renewed church will reform public life. Christian witness reminds government of its accountability to God and empowers the faithful to fulfill their duties as citizens. In teaching us to render to Caesar that which is Caesar's, the Christian Church supports space for political disagreement and debate. It endorses finite patriotism—loyalty without idolatry, criticism without cynicism. The gospel champions the sanctity of human life, urging us to protect the weak, the vulnerable, and the innocent. A robust faith teaches us that the fruits of our labor are a gift from God, to be used for the common good. Spiritual renewal engenders a right ordering of sexuality and family life. A confident orthodoxy fosters care for creation for its own sake and for the sake of human flourishing. Most importantly, even in times of great social crisis, the Lordship of Christ inspires a hope that will not despair.

In our zeal for justice, we must not confuse specific policy proposals for prophetic proclamation, nor collapse the church into a chaplaincy for our favorite political party. Living in a powerful country, we must not exaggerate our ability to influence events for either good or ill. A renewed witness calls for appropriate humility, repentance, and self-criticism.

These are our prayerful and considered responses to the questions that have been posed to us.

Be Steadfast in Faith and Humility

We thank God for the hunger that he has placed in the hearts of people for reform and renewal, for clarity concerning the things of faith, for godly instruction, and holiness in life. We rejoice in our work together for the faithfulness of Christ's church.

We know that along with God's great blessings in the work of the renewal movements come temptations to timidity, faithlessness, and presumption. Our work for renewal involves repentance and amendment of life as well as witness. The empowerment for our ministry comes from abiding in Christ the true vine, apart from whom we can do nothing.

Christ has told his disciples that persecutions will come, but as James reminds us we are to count it all joy when we meet various trials. In that joy, and confident of his great faithfulness, let us together proclaim the Gospel by which we have been saved.

May the grace of our Lord Jesus Christ and the love of God and the fellowship of the Holy Spirit be with you.

Signatories

Presbyterian Church (PCUSA):
Bruce McCormack, Mark Achtemeier, Andrew Purves, Roberta Hestenes, Diogenes Allen

United Methodist Church:
Thomas C. Oden, William Abraham, Leicester Longden, James V. Heidinger II

Episcopalian Church (ECUSA):
Bishop James Stanton, Philip Turner, Ephraim Radner, R. R. Reno

United Church of Christ:
Donald Bloesch

Lutheran Church (ELCA):
Russell Saltzman, Walter Sundberg

American Baptist Church:
Donna Hailson

United Church of Canada:
Victor Shepherd

Notes

Introduction

1. Commentary on Daniel 9:5. The translation is that of William J. Bouwsma, "The Spirituality of John Calvin," in *Christian Spirituality: High Middle Ages and Reformation*, ed. Jill Raitt et al. (New York: Crossroad, 1987), 323.

Chapter 1: The Fellowship of Kindred Minds: Evangelical Identity and the Quest for Christian Unity

1. Grant Wacker, professor at Duke Divinity School, told me this story, which he heard from his dean, Dennis Campbell. Campbell saw this conversation take place at the assembly.

2. Walter J. Hollenweger, "Roman Catholics and Pentecostals in Dialogue," *Ecumenical Review* 51 (April 1999): 147–59; George VanderVelde, "Harare as Evangelical-Ecumenical 'Kairos,' " *Ecumenical Review* 50 (April 1998): 173–83; idem, "Evangelicals and Catholics Together: The Christian Mission in the Third Millennium," *First Things* 43 (May 1994): 15–22.

3. A useful entry point into this conversation is the special issue of the *Christian Scholar's Review* 23 (September 1993), which includes a lead essay by Donald Dayton and responses by George Marsden (whose works Dayton uses as his foil), and also Daniel P. Fuller, Clark H. Pinnock, Douglas A. Sweeney, and Joel A. Carpenter.

4. The foregoing section is a slightly revised version of the first part of my article, "Evangelical Protestantism," in the *Encyclopedia of Religion in the South*, ed. Samuel S. Hill (Macon, Ga.: Mercer University Press, 1984), 239–43.

5. Andrew F. Walls, *The Missionary Movement in Christian History: Studies in the Transmission of Faith* (Maryknoll, N.Y.: Orbis Books, 1996), 81.

6. Ibid., 247.

7. Ibid., 247–53.

8. Richard Lovelace, "Unitive Evangelicalism," chap. 10 of his *Dynamics of Spiritual Life: An Evangelical Theology of Renewal* (Downers Grove, Ill.: InterVarsity Press, 1979), esp. 294–302. Baxter's saying, Lovelace notes (294), comes from continental reformer Rupert Meldenius.

9. See, for example, Carroll Smith-Rosenberg, "Women and Religious Revivals: Anti-ritualism, Liminality, and the Emergence of the American Bourgeoisie," in *The Evangelical Tradition in America*, ed. Leonard I. Sweet (Macon, Ga.: Mercer University Press, 1984), 199–232.

10. Winthrop S. Hudson, *Religion in America*, 4th ed. (New York: Macmillan, 1987), 77–81, here 79.

11. Miroslav Volf, *After Our Likeness: The Church as the Image of the Trinity* (Grand Rapids: Eerdmans, 1998).

12. The single best article on this topic is Dana L. Robert, "Shifting Southward: Global Christianity since 1945," *International Bulletin of Missionary Research* 24 (April 2000): 50–58.

13. This point is George VanderVelde's. See his article, "Harare as Evangelical-Ecumenical 'Kairos,'" cited above.

Chapter 2: What Evangelicals Can Learn from Fundamentalists

1. Harry Emerson Fosdick, "Shall the Fundamentalists Win?" http://www.hyattcarter.com/shall_the_fundamentalists_win.htm.

2. Carl F. H. Henry, *The Uneasy Conscience of Modern Fundamentalism* (Grand Rapids: Eerdmans, 1947), 70.

3. Ockenga, introduction to ibid., 13.

4. Alister McGrath, *Evangelicalism and the Future of Christianity* (Downers Grove, Ill.: InterVarsity Press, 1995), 189.

5. Ibid., 190.

6. Joel A. Carpenter, *Revive Us Again: The Reawakening of American Fundamentalism* (New York: Oxford University Press, 1997), 239–40.

7. See Carnell's chapter on fundamentalism in his *Case for Orthodox Theology* (Philadelphia: Westminster Press, 1959), 113–26.

8. Carpenter, *Revive Us*, 87.

9. For a more detailed discussion of the role that these three themes play in contemporary discussions, see my essay, "Evangelical Ethics," in *Where Shall My Wond'ring Soul Begin? The Landscape of Evangelical Piety and Thought*, ed. Mark A. Noll and Ronald F. Thiemann (Grand Rapids: Eerdmans, 2000), 71–86.

Chapter 3: What's That You Smell? A Fundamentalist Response to *The Smell of Sawdust*

1. Landmark Baptists do not recognize this distinction. Though the number of Landmarkers is small, many consider themselves to be fundamentalists. The Landmark rejection of the universal church has also influenced a few non-Landmark Baptists. Only a minority of Baptist fundamentalists, however, and therefore only a fraction of all fundamentalists, agree with the Landmarkers on this point. Overwhelmingly, fundamentalists affirm the invisible body of Christ as the one, holy, catholic, and apostolic church.

2. To cite one example, the notion of an invisible church was a key to Charles Hodge's ecclesiology. Hodge argued that the idea of an invisible church was an important aspect of evangelical, and not merely Reformed, ecclesiology. He called it the evangelical theory of the church (as opposed to the ritualist and the rationalistic theories). Charles Hodge, "Idea of the Church," *Biblical Repertory and Princeton Review* 25 (April 1853): 249–90; idem, "Theories of the Church," *Biblical Repertory and Princeton Review* 18 (January 1846): 137–58.

3. For Hodge's treatment of the visible church, see his essay, "Visibility of the Church," *Biblical Repertory and Princeton Review* 25 (October 1853): 670–85. Often Baptists do not distinguish the visible church from particular local congregations. While this distinction is important for other reasons, it is not one that fundamentally alters the present argument.

4. Many pedobaptists, of course, include the children of those who profess faith as members of the visible church. While important for a whole series of questions, this inclusion does not greatly change the present argument.

5. For the distinction between doctrinal (theoretical) and practical fundamentals, see Francis Turretin, *Institutes of Elenctic Theology*, trans. George Musgrave Giger, ed. James T. Denniston, Jr., 3 vols. (Phillipsburg, N.J.: Presbyterian and Reformed Publishing, 1992), 1.14.23. On the relationship between doctrine and the affections, see Charles Hodge, "Address to the Students of the Theological Seminary," *Biblical Repertory and Princeton Review* 5, no. 1 (1829): 92.

6. On the importance of this distinction for fundamentalists see Mark Sidwell, *The Dividing Line: Understanding and Applying Biblical Separation* (Greenville, S.C.: Bob Jones University Press, 1998), 42. For a brief but suggestive presentation of a doctrinal calculus from someone who might not wish to identify with fundamentalism, see Robert A. Peterson, "The Case for Traditionalism," in *Two Views of Hell: A Biblical and Theological Dialogue*, ed. Edward William Fudge

and Robert A. Peterson (Downers Grove, Ill.: InterVarsity Press, 2000), 178–79. Peterson's view on this matter approximates the understanding of mainstream fundamentalists.

7. John Theodore Mueller, "A Survey of Luther's Theology: Part I," *Bibliotheca Sacra* 450 (April 1956): 158; Heinrich Schmid, *Doctrinal Theology of the Evangelical Lutheran Church*, trans. Charles A. Hay and Henry E. Jacobs, 3d ed. (n.p.: 1875, 1889; Minneapolis: Augsburg, n.d.), 582–99; Martin I. Klauber, "Calvin on Fundamental Articles and Ecclesiastical Union," *Westminster Theological Journal* 54 (fall 1992): 341–48; idem, *Between Reformed Scholasticism and Pan-Protestantism: Jean-Alphonse Turretin (1671–1737) and Enlightened Orthodoxy at the Academy of Geneva* (Selinsgrove, Pa.: Susquehanna University Press, 1994), throughout; John Calvin, *Institutes of the Christian Religion*, trans. Ford Lewis Battles, ed. John T. McNeill (Philadelphia: Westminster Press, 1960), 4.2.1; James Arminius, *Works of James Arminius: The London Edition*, trans. James Nichols and William Nichols, 3 vols. (vols. 1, 2, London: James Nichols for Longman, Hurst, Rees, Orme, Brown, and Green, 1825, 1828; vol. 3, London: William Nichols for Thomas Baker, 1875; reprint, Grand Rapids: Baker Books, 1986), 1:713–17; Turretin, *Institutes*, 1.14.1–27.

8. Archibald Alexander Hodge, *Outlines of Theology* (New York: Robert Carter and Brothers, 1865; reprint, Carlisle, Pa.: Banner of Truth Trust, 1990), 475–76. This distinction is reflected in Turretin's dictum that some of the essential doctrines must be believed "formally and publicly, as the special and proper objects of faith," while others must be believed "only implicitly and virtually." Some subjects, says Turretin, are fundamental in themselves, while the latter become fundamentals "only accidentally when they run into some fundamental topic" (Turretin, *Institutes*, 1.14.5–9).

9. Calvin, *Institutes*, 4.2.1–2.

10. Arminius, *Works*, 1:417–18.

11. Martin Luther, "The Right and Power of a Christian Congregation or Community to Judge All Teaching and to Call, Appoint, and Dismiss Teachers, Established and Proved from Scripture," trans. A. T. W. Steinhaeuser, in *Works of Martin Luther*, 5 vols. (Philadelphia: Muhlenberg Press, 1931), 4:75.

12. Of course, there have always been a few Christians who have regarded local church membership as an adiaphoron. This attitude appears to have become rather influential in some circles of American evangelicalism during the twentieth century. While not completely absent from fundamentalism, it is much less influential there. Fundamentalists tend to be separatists precisely because they take local church participation seriously. In any case, we should recognize that

those who denigrate the importance of church membership are the ones who have departed from the historic Protestant position.

13. Franz Pieper, *Christian Dogmatics*, 4 vols. (St. Louis: Concordia, 1953), 3:420–21.

14. John H. Gerstner, "When Must a Person Leave a Church?" in *Onward, Christian Soldiers: Protestants Affirm the Church*, ed. Don Kistler (Morgan, Pa.: Soli Deo Gloria Publications, 1999), 283–84.

15. John Miley, *Systematic Theology*, 2 vols. (New York: Eaton and Mains; Cincinnati: Jennings and Pye, 1894), 2:388–89.

16. J. Gresham Machen, "What Should Be Done by Christian People Who Are in a Modernist Church?" *Presbyterian Guardian*, 21 October 1935, 22.

17. J. Gresham Machen, "Are We Schismatics?" *Presbyterian Guardian*, 20 April 1936, 22.

18. Fundamentalists also argue that this is a *biblical* way of looking at the church. I am not trying to make the biblical case for separatism here, though I think that it is compelling. What I am trying to do is to show that the core idea of fundamentalism is a (and perhaps *the*) consistent implementation of the historically Protestant way of viewing the church. Fundamentalists did not invent their categories. They inherited them. When Edward John Carnell accused Machen of "ideological thinking," called him "cultic," and accused him of betraying the Reformed view of the church, he did not take proper account of the Protestant consensus on the visible church. See Carnell, *The Case for Orthodox Theology* (Philadelphia: Westminster Press, 1959), 114–17. For a sustained evaluation of Carnell's criticisms (as well as those offered by others), see my dissertation, "Communion of the Saints: Antecedents of J. Gresham Machen's Separatism in the Ecclesiology of Charles Hodge and the Princeton Theologians" (Ph.D. diss., Dallas Theological Seminary, 2001), throughout. For a discussion of the biblical evidence, see the sources that I suggest for further reading in the final note to this essay.

19. This does not necessarily mean that Christian organizations are always obligated to expel members who are wrestling with fundamental doctrines. There is a difference between a learner who is wrestling with doubts about fundamentals and a teacher who is denying them.

20. There is an old question about when a Christian organization actually becomes apostate. That question is subordinate to my main argument. There is no use asking when an organization becomes apostate unless there is agreement that separation from such an organization is necessary, at whatever point it occurs.

21. The story has been ably told by George M. Marsden in *Reforming Fundamentalism: Fuller Seminary and the New Evangelicalism*,

paperback edition (Grand Rapids: Eerdmans, 1995). This book is widely used in fundamentalist institutions, largely because it confirms so much of what fundamentalists have always said about the New Evangelical agenda.

22. Edward John Carnell, "How My Mind Has Changed," in *How My Mind Has Changed*, ed. Harold E. Fey (Cleveland: Meridian Books, 1961), 101–2.

23. Edward John Carnell, "Christian Fellowship and the Unity of the Church," in *The Case for Biblical Theology*, ed. Ronald H. Nash (Grand Rapids: Eerdmans, 1969), 21–22.

24. Richard J. Mouw, *The Smell of Sawdust* (Grand Rapids: Zondervan, 2000), 105–14. In this chapter, Mouw engages in considerable soul searching over his earlier dismissive attitude toward Roman Catholicism. He focuses his unease on a Catholic schoolteacher who influenced Mouw when she left teaching to become a nun. By the time he was prepared to communicate his respect for her decision, however, she had already died.

25. Edward John Carnell's analysis of Romanism was strikingly similar to that which I present here. "If Christ is an authoritative revelation of the Father's will, Catholicism is anti-Christ. That much is lucidly clear. The gospel according to Christ and the gospel according to Rome cannot, in a rational universe, simultaneously be true. Romanism will fail" (*A Philosophy of the Christian Religion* [Grand Rapids: Eerdmans, 1952], 447–48).

26. President Mouw's selective citing of Charles Hodge does not give the full picture. Hodge viewed the Roman Catholic communion in a binary way: it both was and was not a true church (a part of the visible church) depending upon what one meant by a church. Viewed as the papacy, the Roman church was mystical Babylon and the synagogue of Satan. Only when viewed as a congregation of people could it be called a true church, since the people could sometimes sift the gospel from the official accretions that had been added to it. Romish teachers, he said, do affirm fatal error, and the Council of Trent actually codified fatal doctrines. These observations are set forth in Charles Hodge, "Is the Church of Rome a Part of the Visible Church?" *Biblical Repertory and Princeton Review* 18 (April 1846): 323–30. In his mature *Systematic Theology*, Hodge clarified his understanding of Romanism as a doctrinal system. "The doctrine of the sacrificial character of the eucharist, is an integral part of the great system of error, which must stand or fall as a whole. Romanism is another gospel. It proposes a different method of salvation from that presented in the word of God. . . . This whole theory hangs together. If one assumption is false, the whole is false" (Charles Hodge, *Systematic Theology*,

3 vols. [New York: Scribner, 1872–73; reprint, Grand Rapids: Eerdmans, 1979], 1:135). Hodge's ambivalence reflects that of Turretin, who insisted that Romanism had added anti-Christian doctrines to the Christian fundamentals that it affirmed. Rome was not a true church, but some "remains of the church" existed in it, and God had not wholly left it (Turretin, *Institutes*, 1.14.21, 24; 18.10.11–15; 22–28; 32; 18.13.1–7; 18.14.24; 18.25.10; 19.25.3–7; 19.28.13–14).

27. The NAE statement of faith includes the following articles. It can be located on the National Association of Evangelicals' Web site at http://www.nae.net.

1. We believe the Bible to be the inspired, the only infallible, authoritative Word of God.
2. We believe that there is one God, eternally existent in three persons: Father, Son, and Holy Spirit.
3. We believe in the deity of our Lord Jesus Christ, in His virgin birth, in His sinless life, in His miracles, in His vicarious and atoning death through His shed blood, in His bodily resurrection, in His ascension to the right hand of the Father, and in His personal return in power and glory.
4. We believe that for the salvation of lost and sinful people, regeneration by the Holy Spirit is absolutely essential.
5. We believe in the present ministry of the Holy Spirit by whose indwelling the Christian is enabled to live a godly life.
6. We believe in the resurrection of both the saved and the lost; they that are saved unto the resurrection of life and they that are lost unto the resurrection of damnation.
7. We believe in the spiritual unity of believers in our Lord Jesus Christ.

28. A full-scale theological treatment of ecclesiastical separation remains to be written. The following volumes do make significant contributions, and those who wish to pursue further study on the subject will find them useful: Gary G. Cohen, *Biblical Separation Defended: A Biblical Critique of Ten New Evangelical Arguments* (Phillipsburg, N.J.: Presbyterian and Reformed, 1966); Fred Moritz, *Be Ye Holy: The Call to Christian Separation* (Greenville, S.C.: Bob Jones University Press, 1994); Ernest Pickering, *Biblical Separation: The Struggle for a Pure Church* (Schaumburg, Ill.: Regular Baptist Press, 1979); Mark Sidwell, *The Dividing Line: Understanding and Applying Biblical Separation* (Greenville, S.C.: Bob Jones University Press, 1998).

Chapter 4: The Azusa Street Revival Revisited

1. Leonard Lovett, "The Anti-Pentecostal Movement," in *Aspects of Pentecostal and Charismatic Origins*, ed. Vinson Synan (Plainfield, N.J.: Logos International, 1975), 138.
2. Ibid., 105.
3. Frank Bartleman, *Azusa Street* (1925; repr., New Kensington, Pa.: Whitaker House, 1982), 58–59.
4. Lovett, "Anti-Pentecostal Movement," 138.

Chapter 5: The Pentecostal Vision for Christian Unity

1. For further elaboration, see Richard Shall and Waldo Cesar, *Pentecostalism and the Future of the Christian Church* (Grand Rapids: Eerdmans, 2000).

Chapter 6: Who Is the Holy Spirit for Us Today? The Person and Work of the Holy Spirit in John 20:19–23

1. Gordon Fee, "God's Empowering Presence: The Spirit in Paul's Theology" (audiocassette) (Birmingham, Ala.: Beeson Divinity School, 1993).
2. Jack Hayford, *The Beauty of Spiritual Language: My Journey toward the Heart of God* (Waco, Tex.: Word, 1992), 41.
3. Ibid., 49.
4. Gordon D. Fee, *God's Empowering Presence: The Holy Spirit in the Letters of Paul* (Peabody, Mass.: Hendrickson, 1994), 872.
5. Oswald Chambers, *Biblical Ethics* (CD-ROM) (Hants, England: Marshall, Morgan & Scott, 1997).
6. Barry Seagren, "The Baptism and the Fullness of the Holy Spirit" (audiocassette) (Austin, Tex.: L'Abri Conference, 1986).
7. Brennan Manning, *Reflections for Ragamuffins* (San Francisco: HarperSanFrancisco, 1998), 66.
8. Class notes on Robert Smith, Jr., "Christian Preaching Practicum," Beeson Divinity School, Birmingham, Ala., 30 April 2002.

Chapter 8: The Gospel Call to Common Witness

1. Lukas Vischer and Harding Meyer, eds., *Growth in Agreement Reports and Agreed Statements of Ecumenical Conversations on a World Level* (New York: Paulist Press, 1984), 465–503, http://wcc-coe .org/wcc/what/faith/bem1.html.
2. Faith and Order Commission, *The Nature and Purpose of the*

Church: A Stage on the Way to a Common Statement, paper no. 181 (Geneva: World Council of Churches, 1998), http://wcc-coe.org/wcc/ what/faith/nature1.html.

3. Thomas Rausch, ed., *Catholics and Evangelicals: Do They Share a Common Future?* (Downers Grove, Ill.: InterVarsity Press, 2000).

4. Jeffrey Gros, "Southern Baptists Affirm the Future of Dialogue with the Roman Catholic Church," *Ecumenical Trends* 24, no. 2 (February 1995): 4–6; *Review and Expositor* 79, no. 2 (spring 1982), the theme for which is "Issues in Southern Baptist–Roman Catholic Dialogue"; Jeffrey Gros and Joseph Burgess, eds., *Building Unity* (New York: Paulist Press, 1989), 35–52 (henceforth *BU*); *The Theological Educator*, no. 39 (spring 1989), the theme for which is "To Understand Each Other: Southern Baptists and Roman Catholics"; *Southwestern Journal of Theology* 28, no. 2 (spring 1986), the theme for which is "Grace, Roman Catholic/Southern Baptist Dialogue"; Joseph Burgess and Jeffrey Gros, eds., *Growing Consensus* (New York: Paulist Press, 1995), 557–66 (henceforth *GC*).

5. Southern Baptist–Roman Catholic Conversation, "Report on Sacred Scripture," *Origins* 29 (7 October 1999): 266–68, http://www .usccb.org/seia/southernbaptist.htm.

6. Stephen Duffy, "Southern Baptist and Roman Catholic Soteriologies," *Pro Ecclesia* 9, no. 4 (fall 2000): 434–59.

7. "Summons to Witness to Christ in Today's World: A Report on the Baptist–Roman Catholic International Conversation, 1984–1988," in *Growth in Agreement II,* ed. William Rusch, Harding Meyer, and Jeffrey Gros (Geneva: World Council of Churches, 2000), 373–85.

8. David S. Dockery, ed., *Southern Baptists and American Evangelicals* (Nashville: Broadman & Holman, 1993).

9. Basil Meeking and John Stott, *Evangelical–Roman Catholic Dialogue on Mission* (Grand Rapids: Eerdmans, 1986), also in *GA II* 399–437.

10. World Evangelical Fellowship–Roman Catholic Conversation: 1997, "The Nature and Mission of the Church," *One in Christ* 35, no. 1 (1999): 11–92; "Justification, Scripture, and Tradition: World Evangelical Fellowship–Roman Catholic Dialogue," *Evangelical Review of Theology* 21, no. 2 (April 1997); World Evangelical Fellowship, "A Contemporary Evangelical Perspective on Roman Catholicism," *The Evangelical Review of Theology* 10, no. 4; 11, no. 1 (1986); "World Evangelical Alliance–Pontifical Council for Promoting Christian Unity" and "Church, Evangelization, or Koinonia," *Origins* 33 (16 October 2003): 310–20.

11. Mark A. Noll, *American Evangelical Christianity* (Oxford: Blackwell, 2000).

12. Charles Colson and Richard John Neuhaus, eds., *Evangelicals*

and Catholics Together: Toward a Common Mission (Dallas: Word, 1995). The document was produced in 1994 and published in 1995.

13. Jeffrey Gros, "Evangelical Relations: A Differentiated Catholic Perspective," *Ecumenical Trends* 29, no. 1 (January 2000): 1–9.

14. Donald Bloesch, "Betraying the Reformation?" *Christianity Today*, 7 October 1996, 54–56; Timothy George, introduction to "The Gift of Salvation," *Christianity Today*, 8 December 1997, 34–38; Randy Frame, "Evangelicals, Catholics Issue Salvation Accord," *Christianity Today*, 12 January 1998, 61–63; "A Call to Evangelical Unity: The Gospel of Jesus Christ; An Evangelical Celebration," *Christianity Today*, 14 June 1999, 49–56.

15. *The Lutheran-Catholic Quest for Visible Unity: Harvesting Thirty Years of Dialogue* (Chicago: Evangelical Lutheran Church in America; Washington, D.C.: United States Catholic Conference, 1998).

16. *Joint Declaration on the Doctrine of Justification* (Grand Rapids: Eerdmans, 2000), http://www.elca.org/ea/ecumenical/romancatholic/jddj/jddj.html.

17. Veli-Matti Kärkkäinen, *Spiritus ubi vult spirat: Pneumatology in Roman Catholic–Pentecostal Dialogue (1972–1989)* (Helsinki: Luther-Agricola-Society, 1998). Cf. *GA* 421–32, *GA II* 713–79.

18. *GA II* 753ff. Cf. "Perspectives on *Koinonia*: Final Report of the International Roman Catholic/Pentecostal Dialogue (1985–1989)," *Pneuma* 12, no. 2 (fall 1990): 117–42.

19. Cf. Grant Wacker, *Heaven Below: Early Pentecostals and American Culture* (Cambridge: Harvard University Press, 2001); Walter Hollenweger, *Pentecostalism* (Peabody, Mass.: Hendrickson, 1997).

20. Kilian McDonnell, ed., *Presence, Power, Praise: Documents on the Charismatic Renewal* (Collegeville, Minn.: Liturgical Press, 1980).

21. Terence Crowe, *Pentecostal Unity: Recurring Frustration and Enduring Hopes* (Chicago: Loyola University Press, 1993).

22. Cecil Robeck, "The Society for Pentecostal Studies," *Ecumenical Trends* 14, no. 2 (February 1985): 28–30.

23. John Paul II, "*Ut Unum Sint:* On Commitment to Ecumenism," *Origins* 25, no. 4 (8 June 1995): 49–72, http://www.vatican.va/holy_father/john_paul_ii/encyclicals/documents/hf_jp-ii_enc_25051995_ut-unum-sint_en.html.

Chapter 9: Between the Pope and Billy Graham: Evangelicals and Catholics in Dialogue

1. David Bebbington, "British and American Evangelicalism since

1940," in *Evangelicalism*, ed. Mark A. Noll, David W. Bebbington, and George A. Rawlyk (Oxford: Oxford University Press, 1994), 367.

2. Cited by Cardinal Edward Cassidy in "The Ecumenical Journey towards Unity (Canfield, Ohio: Alba House Cassettes, 1994).

3. "Ut Unum Sint," *Origins* 25, 8 June 1995.

4. Ibid., 54, 58.

5. Cardinal Edward Cassidy, "The Churches and Ecumenism Today," public lecture, Seton Hall University, July 1996. Cardinal Cassidy quotes Dr. Raiser's address in Rome on April 4, 1995, "Thirty Years in the Service of the Ecumenical Movement: The Joint Working Group between the Roman Catholic Church and the World Council of Churches."

6. Joseph Ratzinger, *Church, Ecumenism, and Politics* (New York: Crossroad, 1988), 98.

7. Timothy George, "Catholics and Evangelicals in the Trenches," *Christianity Today*, 16 May 1994, 16.

8. Paul G. Schrotenboer, ed., *Roman Catholicism: A Contemporary Evangelical Perspective* (Grand Rapids: Baker, 1998), 8–13.

9. Ibid., 25.

10. Unpublished paper by Jeffrey Gros, "*Dignitatis Humanae* and Ecumenism: A Foundation and a Promise," March 1993, 8.

11. *First Things* 79 (January 1998): 20–23. "The Gift of Salvation" also appeared in the December 1997 issue of *Christianity Today*.

12. *Your Word Is Truth: A Project of Evangelicals and Catholics Together*, ed. Charles Colson and Richard John Neuhaus (Grand Rapids: Eerdmans, 2002).

13. Ibid., xii.

Chapter 10: Ecumenical and Evangelical: Mutual Affirmation and Admonition

1. Thus, "the modern ecumenical movement . . . is most commonly traced to the World Mission Conference in Edinburgh in 1910" (Leon Howell, *Acting in Faith: The World Council of Churches since 1975* [Geneva: World Council of Churches, 1982], 3). For an early theological primer and historical account, see J. Robert Nelson, *One Lord, One Church* (New York: Association Press, 1958).

2. For the theological basis and "covenanting proposal," see *Churches in Covenant Communion* and *The COCU Consensus*, combined edition (Princeton, N.J.: Consultation on Church Union, 1995).

3. See Gabriel Fackre and Michael Root, *Affirmations and Admonitions: Lutheran Decision and Dialogue with Reformed, Episcopal,*

and Roman Catholic Churches (Grand Rapids: Eerdmans, 1998); William Rusch, ed., *Ecumenical Perspectives on the Joint Declaration* (Collegeville, Minn.: Liturgical Press, 2001).

4. I explain the identity in *Ecumenical Faith in Evangelical Perspective* (Grand Rapids: Eerdmans, 1993). My working definition of *evangelical* is that found in my entry, "Evangelical, Evangelicalism," in *The Westminster Dictionary of Christian Theology* (Philadelphia: Westminster Press, 1983), 191–92.

5. On the concept, see Keith F. Nickle and Timothy F. Lull, eds., *A Common Calling: The Witness of Our Reformation Churches in North America Today* (Minneapolis: Augsburg Fortress, 1993), 8, 30, 39–40, 66, 67.

6. Harding Myer, "A Common Calling in Relation to International Agreements," *Ecumenical Trends* 23, no. 8 (September 1994): 116.

7. Philip Yancey, "Fixing Our Weakest Link," *Christianity Today*, 9 July 2001, 64.

8. *Joint Declaration on the Doctrine of Justification* (Grand Rapids: Eerdmans, 2000), 15–27.

9. See "Agreement between Reformation Churches in Europe (Leuenberg Agreement)," in *An Invitation to Action: The Lutheran-Reformed Dialogue*, ed. James E. Andrews and Joseph A. Burgess, ser. 3 (Minneapolis: Fortress Press, 1984), 65–73.

10. Pentecostal, Roman Catholic, ecumenical, evangelical, and fundamentalist traditions being the interlocutors.

11. As in the *Joint Declaration on Justification* and also "The Gift of Salvation: Evangelicals and Catholics Together," *Christianity Today*, 8 December 1997, 35–38.

12. Gabriel Fackre, ed., *Judgment Day at the White House* (Grand Rapids: Eerdmans, 1999).

13. Ethics and Public Policy Center, "Evangelicals and Political Power: Lessons from the Past, Lessons for the Future," 2 February 2001.

14. As in Stanley Hauerwas and William H. Willimon, *Resident Aliens: Life in a Christian Colony* (Nashville: Abingdon Press, 1989).

15. "The Theological Declaration of Barmen," in *The Church's Confession Under Hitler*, ed. Arthur Cochrane (Philadelphia: Westminster Press, 1962), 237.

16. "An Evangelical Mega-Shift? The Promise and Peril of an 'Open' View of God," *The Christian Century*, 3 May 1995, 484–87.

17. Stanley J. Grenz, *Renewing the Center: Evangelical Theology in a Post-theological Era* (Grand Rapids: Baker, 2000), 46–77.

18. Karl Barth, *Church Dogmatics* IV/2, trans. and ed. G. W. Bromiley and T. F. Torrance (Edinburgh: T & T Clark, 1958), 112–13.

19. Karl Barth, *Church Dogmatics*, IV/1, trans. G. W. Bromiley (Edinburgh: T & T Clark, 1956), 150.

20. As examined in my *Ecumenical Faith in Evangelical Perspective*, 130–33.

21. See Karl Barth, *Church Dogmatics* IV/3/1, trans. and ed. G. W. Bromiley and T. F. Torrance (Edinburgh: T & T Clark, 1961), 477–78.

22. Of course, these kinds of self-criticism are made also from within evangelical ranks, as in David F. Well's *No Place for Truth: Or Whatever Happened to Evangelical Theology?* (Grand Rapids: Eerdmans, 1993).

23. See Philip Schaff, *The Principle of Protestantism*, trans. John W. Nevin, ed. Bard Thompson and George H. Bricker (Philadelphia: United Church Press, 1964), 80–97.

24. These issues are explored in Gabriel Fackre, *The Religious Right and Christian Faith* (Grand Rapids: Eerdmans, 1982).

25. "Three Types of Theology Today," *The Clergy Journal*, November–December 2001.

26. See *Church Dogmatics*, IV/3/1, 97, 115, 118, 119, 125.

27. Time and space preclude all the admonitions that might be given to evangelicals by ecumenicals. For example, the question must be asked why the right stress on the priority of Scripture in the evangelical structure of authority has too often eventuated in a biblicism that overrides the carefully researched results of the physical sciences, as in the insistence by a camp of evangelicals on a literal six-day scenario of the world's origins. Lacking here is a doctrine of common grace ready to appropriate the results of validated scientific inquiry because of a radical interpretation of the *sola scriptura* that precludes the ministerial (not magisterial) role of both tradition and the modest deliverances of human experience, rational, moral, and affective. See my *Doctrine of Revelation: A Narrative Interpretation* (Grand Rapids: Eerdmans, 1997). For another set of critiques of evangelicalism from a sympathetic observer and co-belligerent, see Elizabeth Achtemeier, *Not Til I Have Done: A Personal Testimony* (Louisville: Westminster John Knox, 1999), 121–22.

28. *Man's Disorder and God's Design: The Amsterdam Assembly Series* (New York: Harper & Bros., 1948).

29. The characterizations are Barth's in *Church Dogmatics*, IV/3/1, 94–165.

30. As delineated in my *Christian Story*, 3d ed., vol. 1 (Grand Rapids: Eerdmans, 1996), 13–26.

31. As in Gibson Winter, *The New Creation as Metropolis* (New York: Macmillan, 1963), and in the series interpreting a World Council of Churches study, by Colin Williams, *Where in the World?* (New

York: National Council of Churches, 1963) and *What in the World?* (New York: National Council of Churches, 1964). For an analysis and critique, see my "The Crisis of the Congregation: A Debate," in *Voluntary Associations: A Study of Groups in Free Societies* (Richmond, Va.: John Knox Press, 1966), 275–97.

32. See the representative work by Orlando Costas, *Liberating News: A Theology of Contextual Evangelization* (Grand Rapids: Eerdmans, 1989), and my *Word in Deed: Theological Themes in Evangelism* (Grand Rapids: Eerdmans, 1975).

33. For a spectrum of points of view, see the scrutiny in *The Christian Story*, 53–59.

34. As in Mary Stewart Van Leeuwen, ed., *After Eden: Facing the Challenge of Gender Reconciliation* (Grand Rapids: Eerdmans, 1993).

35. See the *Interpretation* issue devoted to that subject, "The Church at the Center," vol. 51, no. 2 (April 1997).

36. For what this might mean see the book on the subject by the "Confessing Christ" movement, *How Shall We Sing the Lord's Song?* ed. Richard Christensen (Pittsburgh: Pickwick Press, 1997).

37. Interestingly, a Roman Catholic journal asked just this question. See *New Theology Review*, vol. 1, no. 2 (May 1988), and my article, "Positive Witness and Honorable Intentions," 58–73.

38. There is a twenty-year history of "evangelical-liberal" dialogue sponsored by the Massachusetts Council of Churches that points toward what might be done, though "liberal" does not describe the "ecumenical" I am discussing here.

Chapter 11: Can Anything Good Come Out of Liberalism? One Pilgrim's Regress

This essay includes sections also found in my *Rebirth of Orthodoxy: Signs of Life in Christianity* (San Francisco: HarperSanFrancisco, 2003), which was published after this talk was delivered in Birmingham in 2002.

1. Am I thankful that my life, my whole ministry, has come out of liberalism? "Come out" is an ambiguous phrase, which can either imply coming out as a negation of the previous pattern, or going beyond as a positive development. When I "came out"—as an orthodox Catholic evangelical within Methodism—it required a lot of explaining to my curious liberal friends.

2. Alfred North Whitehead, *Adventures of Ideas* (New York: The Free Press, 1967), 170.

3. H. Richard Niebuhr, *The Kingdom of God in America* (New York: Harper & Row, 1937), 193.

4. Walter Marshall Horton, *Realistic Theology* (New York: Harper, 1934), 8–9.

5. Autobiographical narrative is a familiar genre within classic Christianity, best epitomized by Gregory Nazianzen's *Flight to Pontus* and Augustine's *Confessions*. There are many examples of the genre of biography in the orthodox tradition of Athanasius's *Life of Anthony*, Jerome's *Lives*, Chrysostom's feast-day homilies, Theodoret's *A History of the Monks of Syria*, and Gregory the Great's *Dialogues*. So also are there many recent expressions of how orthodox faith has changed personal lives. This genre has been refashioned in our time by Malcolm Muggeridge, Aleksandr Solzhenitsyn, Lesslie Newbigin, and Richard Neuhaus. The personal narratives of Peter Toon, Dallas Willard, Paul Vitz, Charles Colson, Peter Gilquist, and Tom Howard are moving. They tell the story of the power of classic Christianity to transform modern lives. Biographical skills have been powerfully honed in recent years by George Weigel, Will Willimon, Andrew Walker, Keith Fournier, and Brad Nassif.

6. Many of my revolutionary mentors were socialists or quasi-Marxists: Josef Hromadka, Herbert Marcuse, Paul Tillich, and Jean-Paul Sartre. Much of my social ideology before the Vietnam War was formed around the group that wrote the Port Huron Statement. This group was to influence the founding of the Students for Democratic Action and the Students for a Democratic Society, including Tom Hayden, Richard Shaull, Carl Zimmerman, and company.

7. Like Henry Ward, Kirby Page, David Soper, and G. Bromily Oxnam, and existentialists like Joseph Mathews.

8. I went to Yale more than a decade before Senator Clinton did, but we had many threads of mutual friends, and almost a total congruence of values in those days. Her former pastor and mentor, Professor Don Jones, remains my close colleague in ethics at Drew University. Methodist social liberalism taught me how to advocate liberalized abortion and early feminism almost a decade before the works of Germaine Greer and Rosemary Ruether further raised my consciousness. During her years in the White House, Clinton belonged to one of the most politically radical local congregations among United Methodists.

9. I was freed to ask: How can God have become truly human without ceasing to be God? How could this one die for my sins? How could human freedom, when so distorted by the history of sin, become radically atoned in the cross? If God is almighty and all good, how could God allow sin to have such a persistent hold on human social processes? How can the incomprehensible God make himself sufficiently known to finite human minds? If God is Father, God is Son, and God is Holy Spirit, how is God one? How can the faithful proxi-

mately refract the holiness of God within the history of sin? How can the church manifest the holiness of the people of God and at the same time engage in the transformation of the world? Not a new question in the list, nor a dull one.

Chapter 12: Up the Creek: Paddling in the Maelstrom of the Mainline

1. (P)ECUSA is the proper acronym because the legal title of the church still includes the word *Protestant.* Most Episcopalians today, however, do not realize this. Thus ECUSA has become the usual form.

Chapter 14: Renewal in the Mainline: An Evangelical Outsider's Perspective

1. *Emerging Trends* (Princeton Religion Research Center) 23, no. 9 (December 2001).
2. Taken from "Slain Missionaries Defining Moment for Layman Editor" (27 July 1998) in *The Presbyterian Layman,* available online at www.layman.org.
3. Ibid.
4. From the Web site of The Institute on Religion and Democracy at www.ird-renew.org. Go to the "Association for Church Renewal" link.
5. Ibid.

Contributors

John H. Armstrong
Director, Reformation and Revival Ministries
Carol Stream, Illinois

Kevin T. Bauder
Associate Professor of Theology, Central Baptist Seminary
Plymouth, Minnesota

Joel A. Carpenter
Provost, Calvin College
Grand Rapids, Michigan

Glenn E. Davis
Canon Theologian, Diocese of Alabama
International Communion of the Charismatic Episcopal
    Church
Rector, Lamb of God Charismatic Episcopal Church
Pelham, Alabama

Gabriel Fackre
Abbot Professor of Christian Theology Emeritus, Andover
    Newton Theological School
Boston, Massachusetts

Timothy George
Dean, Beeson Divinity School
Samford University
Birmingham, Alabama

Jeffrey Gros
Associate Director, Secretariat for Ecumenical and
    Interreligious Affairs
National Conference of Catholic Bishops, United States
    Catholic Conference
Washington, D.C.

Cheryl Bridges Johns
Professor of Discipleship and Christian Formation, Church of
    God Theological Seminary
Cleveland, Tennessee

Diane Knippers
President, Institute on Religion and Democracy
Washington, D.C.

George D. McKinney
Bishop, Southern California Second Ecclesiastical
    Jurisdiction, Church of God in Christ
Pastor, St. Stephen's Church of God in Christ
Los Angeles, California

Richard J. Mouw
President and Professor of Christian Philosophy, Fuller
    Theological Seminary
Pasadena, California

Richard John Neuhaus
President, The Institute on Religion and Public Life
New York, New York

Thomas C. Oden
Henry Anson Buttz Professor of Theology and Ethics
Drew University
Madison, New Jersey

Paul F. M. Zahl
Dean, Cathedral Church of the Advent
Birmingham, Alabama

Index